NORTH EASTERN STEAM

1. No 701 (Class VI) on the Plain of York near Beningbrough

NORTH EASTERN STEAM

W. A. Tuplin

London
GEORGE ALLEN & UNWIN LTD
RUSKIN HOUSE   MUSEUM STREET

FIRST PUBLISHED IN 1970

© *George Allen & Unwin Ltd 1970*

SBN 04 385051 0

PRINTED IN GREAT BRITAIN
in 12 on 13pt Bembo type
BY BLACKFRIARS PRESS

PREFACE

A S the object of a railway was to make a profit by transporting
goods and passengers, the North Eastern Railway was proof
against all criticizm; that it succeeded admirably is shown for
example by the 1922 dividend of 7½ per cent on its ordinary
shares with the next best in the LNER group (the Great Northern)
at 4 per cent. Although this is not proof of special efficiency in
the locomotive department of the North Eastern Railway, it
does suggest that there was not much wrong with it and makes
an author less chary than he might otherwise be of hazarding
opinions on matters of detail.

Highly divergent views are held on the subject of external
beauty of locomotives but that is not a reason for suppressing
them. To the writer's eye the North Eastern was transformed in
this respect by the coming of T. W. Worsdell, and that event
marks the beginning of the period examined in this book. The
bare bones of the history (official figures) have been exposed
many times and although they are neither exciting nor precisely
significant some are repeated in this book as a concession to
convention and as a possible convenience. More important and
more interesting is the story of development of design and performance. Its details may be appreciated in different ways and it
seems unlikely that there will ever be a last word about it.

Because the appeal of the steam locomotive is basically emotional, it varies widely between observers and so there is justification for personal reminiscences about its work in particular
places at particular times. Some notes of this kind are ventured
here in addition to examination of technical features of North
Eastern locomotives and their running.

An interesting harvest could be gleaned from enginemen's

gossip even after the apparently airy-fairy tales had been win-
nowed out of it. In this field, however, no story should be
questioned on the mere ground of its improbability. The steam
locomotive as a traffic machine was sometimes criticized as being
unpredictable. It was, however, stolid compared with some of
the many human beings concerned in its design, manufacture and
operation, and official records of what happened to locomotives
in service represent only a small fraction of the full story. This
circumstance is not peculiar to the operation of locomotives or
of railways. In every organization there are irresistible reasons
why official records are liable to be incomplete and incorrect.
Keen observers are aware of this and so are not persuaded to dis-
believe what they have seen just because the official account is
different. Reproduction of official figures (even with rational
'rounding off') in this book is not to be taken as specific endorse-
ment of them.

The writer is indebted in some degree to most of the authors
of published work about North Eastern locomotives and particular instances are too numerous for individual acknowledgement
except for one outstanding case. This is an unsigned article of
remarkably comprehensive character in the *Railway Magazine*
for June 1910. The files of the *Railway Magazine*, of *The Locomotive*, of *The Engineer* and of *Engineering* contain the majority
of the sources used in preparing this book.

Special mention is gratefully made of enthusiastic assistance by
Mr. W. J. MacDonald, archivist in charge of British Railways
Historical Records and Documents, housed in the ex-North
Eastern Railway's General Offices at York.

The publications of the Railway Correspondence and Travel
Society have been useful in checking up on building dates and
certain technical details.

The frontispiece and Figs 26 and 28 appear by courtesy of
Messrs Real Photographs Ltd. while Fig 49 is from a photograph
taken by Mr. Newman C. Johnson and reproduced in *The
Railway Magazine* for May 1934. Figs 50 and 51 appear by courtesy
of British Railways. The remaining photographic illustrations are
mostly derived from North Eastern Railway official photographs.

NOTE ON NOTATION

IN this book the wheel-arrangement of any locomotive is indicated in the usual way by the numbers of wheels in each of three
groups. Unless the locomotive has no outside cylinders the figures
for wheel arrangement are preceded by a figure which is the
number of cylinders in the engine.

The letter C preceding the symbols for wheel-arrangement
denotes an engine with compound expansion.

The letter T after the wheel-arrangement denotes an engine
with side-tanks.

CT denotes a tank engine with a crane.

ST indicates a saddle-tank engine.

WT indicates a well-tank engine.

Thus 0–6–0   represents an engine with six coupled wheels and
no others, and with two inside cylinders and no
others.

    C/0–6–0   means a 0–6–0 built as a two-cylinder compound.

    4C/4–4–2   means a four-cylinder compound 'Atlantic'

    C/0–6–2T means a two-cylinder compound engine with
side-tanks.

When referring in general terms to locomotives of any
particular wheel-arrangement the prefix may be omitted.

CONTENTS

TABLES

ILLUSTRATIONS

FIGURES

CHAPTER I

INTRODUCTORY

⸻

·THE territory of the North Eastern Railway was bounded by the England–Scotland border on the north, by the Midland Railway's Leeds–Carlisle main line on the west, by the North Eastern's own line from Leeds to Hull on the south and by the North Sea on the east. There were a few limbs extending outside that area as, for example, the York–Doncaster main line as far as Shaftholme Junction four miles north of Doncaster, but no other railway penetrated the area apart from the Hull & Barnsley Railway line between Howden and Hull.

The principal passenger train routes were

(a) the 'East Coast' main line from Shaftholme Junction through Selby, York and Newcastle to Berwick-on-Tweed;

(b) Leeds to Newcastle via Harrogate, Northallerton and Sunderland;

(c) Leeds to Scarborough via York;

(d) Leeds to Hull;

(e) York to Burton Salmon and thence to Sheffield or Normanton;

(f) Newcastle to Carlisle.

North Eastern engines worked the East Coast trains between Berwick and Edinburgh over the North British Railway.

The principal goods train routes followed the same general pattern. The area of heaviest traffic, passenger and goods, was bounded by the River Tees and the River Tyne, for there were the coal mines, heavy industry and ports. A long, steeply-graded branch extended from Bishop Auckland over Stainmore Summit to Tebay on the North Western main line. Coke was taken to Barrow-in-Furness by this route and iron ore brought back.

The following figures (give or take a few per cent) refer to the North Eastern Railway on its absorption into the LNER at the end of 1922.

Number of locomotives	2150*
Number of coaches and the like	4000
Number of goods vehicles	124000
Number of service vehicles	4000
Route mileage	1870
Track mileage	5400
Number of staff	63000

From 1885, development of locomotive design on the North Eastern was steady and orderly. Engines were shapely, dignified and predominantly green. Safety-valves were encased in graceful brass; between 1900 and 1911 chimneys appeared with brass rims. Most of the engines were 'good go-ers' and some indeed were 'flyers'. This book takes a look at them and their work.

As whole books have been written about British Railways standard locomotives limited to nine classes with many common features designed with the background of more than a century's experience with steam locomotives, it is clear that no single volume can deal exhaustively with North Eastern locomotives of which there were over sixty classes and hundreds of detail variations. In this book a consecutive account is attempted of North Eastern locomotives produced after about 1885 when some semblance of logical development can be discerned to have begun. One detail of it was unusual and very convenient. T. W. Worsdell called his first design Class A and the class-letter of every subsequent design was the next in the alphabet after that of its predecessor. There was an obvious limit to this procedure but it was only on the development of Raven's 3/4-4-4T in 1913 that the North Eastern produced a locomotive that needed a class-letter after Z. On January 1, 1923 the North Eastern became part of the LNER group and its Class 4-6-2 became Class A2 in the new series of class-letters introduced by the group.

*Including those absorbed from the Hull & Barnsley Railway.

Before 1885, North Eastern locomotive stock had such apparently endless variety in details of many kinds that it was in one sense a classless society. Almost every engine had a special feature of some kind but most of the variations had no technical significance. There were, however, a few pre-Worsdell designs that were distinctive in potentially valuable ways even though the North Eastern made no immediate development of them. Two of these were due to William Bouch, locomotive engineer of the Stockton & Darlington Railway which was amalgamated with the North Eastern (which dated from 1854) in 1863.

The first design was that of a pair of outside-cylinder 4–4–0s *Brougham* and *Lowther* built in 1860 for running passenger trains over the 1369 ft high Stainmore summit between Barnard Castle and Kirkby Stephen. Probably because of the special inclemencies of North of England weather at such altitudes, Bouch provided the engines with what were incomparably the most commodious cabs ever seen on a British locomotive up to that time. And, what was the response of the enginemen to such unimagined comfort? Marked opposition! They did not like being closed in. (Were they nomads who never slept under a roof?) They would get pneumonia or dyspepsia or toothache if they were to ride in such cabs in cold weather and it would be too hot in the summer. Nothing arouses resentful suspicion in the average workman so certainly as an attempt to do him a good turn. Over forty years later Churchward built a side-window cab on a Great Western locomotive but the grumblings were so grievous that he soon had it taken off again and cab-comfort disappeared from the Swindon list of things that needed looking into.

It is unusual in industrial relations for the reason specified for a grievance to be the real one. One wonders whether the objectors to Bouch's fine cab were fearful of being regarded by less fortunate enginemen as 'soft' if they accepted the invitation to take cover.

Be that as it may, Bouch responded by restricting 'protection' in the somewhat similar 'Saltburn' Class (1862) to a roofless, sideless, weatherboard no higher than the chin of an average driver standing upright on the footplate.

Historically *Brougham* was of interest as being the first outside-cylinder 4–4–0 to run in Britain. The 'Saltburns' were notable in having 7 ft wheels nearly touching one another. Such large wheels for use on a railway where there was neither need nor opportunity for fast running have surprised successive generations of commentators. The baseless belief that big wheels could not pull hard at low speed still persisted a hundred years after Bouch built *Saltburn*. Nine years after that event he relented a little from his extreme reaction to the enginemen's objection to cabs and on yet another design of two-cylinder 4–4–0, No 238, he erected a compromise cab of an elemental form in which the side sheets, narrowed above waist-level, were bent over towards each other to form a flat roof. But this was a detail of no technical importance compared with certain dimensions that suggested some original thought by the designer.

First of all the piston-stroke of 30 inches was longer than any other ever used in Great Britain except on the Great Western Railway. There is no special magic in 30 inches or in any other number of inches. The point was that the ratio of piston-stroke to cylinder-diameter (17 inches) was distinctly higher than the usual ratio, in contemporary British locomotives, of 24 to 18. A high value of this ratio corresponds to a low value of the ratio of clearance volume to volume swept by the piston and offers the possibility of using a high expansion ratio and thereby raising the cylinder-efficiency. (It must be admitted that the possible gain in this respect is not great, but 30 years later Churchward standardized 30-inch stroke of the Great Western with this in mind).

No. 238 had piston valves 13 inches in diameter, very much larger than usual in relation to cylinder volume and indeed larger than any other ever used in a British locomotive. This suggests that Bouch had realized that valves in many conventional engines were not so large as they might usefully be, but in No. 238 he probably went too far in the opposite direction. Excessively large valves waste steam at low speed by letting steam quickly out of the cylinders at times when a slower escape would enable it to do more work on the pistons.

Bouch hopefully made valve-heads in the form of plain cylinders and, moreover, in brass so that they might slide easily on the cast iron that formed the valve-chests. But with rise in temperature brass expands (or tries to expand) distinctly more than does iron or steel. This means that if the valve fits the valve chest nicely when hot, it will allow steam to leak past it when the metal is cold. This is not really a serious matter because the metal does not long remain cold with steam blowing past it, but unless the sliding members are made with the appropriate difference in diameter they will tend to 'seize' when hot. In fact the 238 Class did give trouble with valves 'seizing' in the valve-chests and this was never completely overcome. In locomotive practice it was never possible to maintain any close approximation to steam-tightness unless each valve-head had some flexibility to accommodate itself to the various diameter-changes made by wear of the sliding surfaces.

The circumstances were similar to those that bedevilled operation of rotary valves in Paget's 2–6–2 built at Derby forty years later and of sleeve-valves in Bulleid's 'Leader' Class 0–6–6–0 some eighty years later.

But the 238 Class were in additional trouble as, by all accounts, Bouch made no provision against the dangers arising from the trapping of water in the cylinders and so cylinder-covers were burst far more frequently than would have been the case had the engines had the usual flat valves.

The weight of the front of the engine was taken through the thin floor of the smokebox to a vertical pin extending downwards for about 49 inches with a spherical end about 9 inches in diameter. This rested on the spherical bottom of a 10-in. deep hole in the central member of the bogie frame. The bogie could thus swivel in any direction about the centre of the sphere and was therefore able to accommodate curvature of the track and local vertical irregularities in it. It had no side-movement relative to the main frame except in so far as flexing of the smokebox-floor could allow the spherical bottom end of the bogie-pin to move sideways. There was nothing but gravity to stop the bogie-pin from jumping up out of its socket on the bogie.

The firebox had a longitudinal 'water-wall' extending vertically between fire-grate level and that of the bottom of the boiler barrel. There were consequently two separate fires fed through a single hole. There was no brick-arch or fire-hole deflector plate and so the engines most probably burned coke; coal would have produced far too much smoke.

For most of their length forward from the fire-box the tubes were straight but in the last foot or so they were bent so as to slope *downwards* in the approach to the front tube-plate.

In the cab was a reversing lever of the usual type but it latched, not into a notched sector, but into a barrel-shaped screw with a hand-wheel. So a strong man in a hurry would reverse the engine by hands applied to the lever; at the other extreme, fine adjustment of cut-off could be made by turning the hand-wheel. Frequent use of the second method would cause rapid wear of either the screw or the necessarily small latch because force was transmitted from either to the other through a very small area with sliding contact.

In the 238 Class there was an abrupt rise in the running board abreast of the front of the smokebox, and a further rise near the front sand-box to clear the coupling rods in the top half of their revolution. Over the length of the engine the valance beneath the running board extended down to the level of the piston rod, so that the crosshead and slide bars were out of sight. The deep valance abreast of the coupling rod had two long slots and the driving wheel splasher was pierced by a crescent-moon-shaped slot. Or on some engines the valance had four long slots separated only by three narrow webs, while the splasher was so be-slotted radially that only narrow ligaments connected the rim to the centre.

One feels that the tortured sheeting expressed the Victorian instinct to hide things tempered by a practical man's conviction that it might be useful to see them occasionally.

The 'Broughams' and the 'Saltburns' had flared-top chimneys in ordinary Victorian styles but No 238 and her nine sisters had stove-pipe chimneys as in Fletcher practice. This never developed beyond 2–4–0s for passenger trains except for the ten 'Whitby bogies'. These were inside-cylinder 4–4–0s but they looked strange because the leading axle was vertically beneath the chimney instead of being in the usual position ahead of the smokebox.

The basic concept of the 'Whitby bogie' seems to have been that of a 2–4–0 modified to cope with the abnormal curvatures of the Pickering–Whitby line. A very short bogie was placed with its centre where the leading axle of the corresponding 2–4–0 would have been. The general form of the locomotive was that of a moderately conventional double-frame 4–4–0 after having run into some obstruction that had pushed the bogie back, but was not high enough to be hit by the buffers. Crew protection at the front was limited to a low weather-board but reconstruction in the later 1880s included a typical Fletcher cab and much enlarged front sand-boxes.

The original bogies had conventional inside plate frames, but later on some at least of the bogie axles were replaced by longer ones with outside axle-boxes loaded by inverted laminated springs.

Passengers on the Pickering–Whitby line were less lucky than the locomotives as many years had to elapse after the building of the 'Whitby-bogie' locomotives before any bogie-coach appeared on that route. Four-wheel vehicles (one would feel uneasy about calling them coaches) were usual and were small enough to be called 'Whitby bathing-machines' after the four-wheel wooden huts that were common on bathing-beaches in Victorian Britain as accommodation for the operations of changing into bathing dress and back again. Certain Great Northern main-line trains included four-wheel coaches running between King's Cross and Whitby and any passenger who travelled in one at high Great Northern speed from York to London might feel that he needed another holiday immediately.

The use, forty years later, of 4–6–2T tank engines on the Pickering–Whitby line inclines one to believe that Fletcher's evident respect for the curvature of that line was perhaps a little excessive.

Like many other North Eastern locomotives of the period, the 'Whitby-bogies' in their original form had each a raised fire-box with the top sheet still further raised in the middle as if to form a seating for a safety-valve although none was there. The initial safeguard against excessive boiler-pressure was a Salter safety-valve on a huge coarsely-curved dome but in this field there is sense in the 'belt and braces' policy and so an additional safety-valve was afterwards mounted on the outer fire-box.

Whatever may be said or imagined about the quality of performance of North Eastern engines running in the Fletcher period (and it is impossible now to assess the only significant ratio which is cost per unit of work done) one must regret their common crudity in appearance, and their unanimous defiance of any aesthetic principles discernible in the externals of contemporary steam locomotives. This is written without any suggestion of criticism. An important function—perhaps the main function—of the North Eastern Railway was to provide a cheap vital link between the operation of separating coal from the water under the earth and that of burning it where it would do some good. The North Eastern did this with 10 per cent dividend but there was nothing pretty about it and no useful purpose would have been served by trying to make the locomotives pretty even if anyone had thought of it, or even if anyone could define 'pretty' to the satisfaction of anyone else. The general impression one forms from examination of photographs of these highly variegated engines is that each of them was put together by a group of eighteenth-century veterans, benign old craftsmen who made a good engine out of a lot of miscellaneous scrap but who felt too modest about their product to restrain any apprentice fairground-decorator from slapping paint on it.

To the writer the locomotives attributed to Bouch and Fletcher exhibit a unique primordial crudity; it is epitomized in the shape of the Bouch regulator handle still to be seen on the 'long-boiler' 0-6-0 No 1275 in York Museum.

The unhappy outward appearance of most of the engines did not prevent them from doing their jobs of pulling trains and holding them back but black paint would have been no detriment. The garish colours and blatant lining out (or 'banding out') of most of those engines flaunted Victorian taste at its lowest level, unless indeed that was expressed in what was done to Fletcher 2-4-0 No 363 in decorating it for the Stephenson Centenary celebrations in 1881. One wonders whether it could have looked as bad as the photographs suggest.

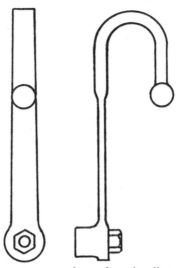

Fig 1 Bouch regulator handle

Immediately after one has examined the Tennant 2–4–0 in York Museum, sight of the Fletcher 2–4–0 suggests that it is an elaborate three-dimensional caricature contrived to show in horrid technicolour how frightful a conventional steam locomotive can be made to look by someone who knows how to set about it. Some of the enginemen sought to allay the general visual horror of North Eastern engines by adding local decorations of their own. One of these, swiftly suppressed after it had caught a high official eye at York, was an early exposition of the present world-wide practice in factories and workshops of pinning up pictures of near-nudes. The same subject inspired many of the 'doodlings' made at North Eastern directors' meetings in the 1870s in a book of rough notes still to be seen in the archives at York.

Fascinating though such details may make the work of historians who would try to produce a fully detailed account of North Eastern locomotives in pre-Worsdell days, space limitation precludes more than a brief mention of them in this book. Its main subject is examination of the orderly development of North Eastern steam in respectable-looking locomotives by T. W. Worsdell and his successors but it may be useful first of all to take a look at the immediately preceding conditions.

23

CHAPTER 2

SURVEY OF SIX REIGNS

Edward Fletcher

EDWARD Fletcher, born in 1809, spent all his long working life in running, building and designing railway locomotives or in supervising those who did so. From 1854 till his retirement at the age of 74 he was responsible for all locomotive matters of the North Eastern Railway. It built locomotives at works at Gateshead, York and Leeds, each with its own supervising engineer who was in charge of design and production and was not officially required to collaborate with his 'opposite numbers'. With plenty of business originating in its own territory and no competitor to try to get any of it the North Eastern could pay a 10 per cent dividend without any need for economy drives or scientific management or reorganization. Things ran smoothly and satisfactorily without any technical discipline, with supervisory staff going every one to his own way and nobody bothering anybody else. The possibility of saving money by standardizing the smallest number of different designs incorporating the smallest number of different components had never occurred to anyone on the North Eastern. Among the locomotives, identical twins were rarities even in nominally identical classes but in spite of all the wasteful consequences of this state of affairs the shareholders were kept happy and nothing was done to make the company's servants unhappy. So there was little to be gained from stirring up these placid waters by asking questions or giving new orders. Fletcher realized this, refrained from prodding anyone and became a benign father-figurehead of the locomotive department. He naturally gained the affectionate regard of those of his staff who knew he was there. What surer way was there of achieving this happy condition than that of pursuing a consistent policy of non-interference? None at all! Successful organizations are successful largely because of unofficial collaboration and covering-up at low levels. The less interference of high-level officials with technical details the better. These were the conditions in the locomotive department of the North Eastern when Fletcher retired in 1882.

Alexander McDonnell

These were the conditions that shocked his successor McDonnell when he surveyed his new charge of 1400 locomotives soon after his arrival at Gateshead. He had come from the Great Southern & Western Railway Works at Inchicore in Ireland where he had gained valuable experience in overdue rationalization of manufacture and maintenance of locomotives. He found a similar but much larger task awaiting him on the North Eastern, and made confident by his success in Ireland began a big job of 'cleaning up' the organization and its methods. All that was required to energize anyone in reorganization of this sort was an innate active hatred of waste. Some people do hate waste but many others passively tolerate it because they don't recognize it. Long bother-free years under Fletcher would inevitably produce resentful suspicion of his successor whoever he might be, but when he had arrived and had started some reforms, antagonism at once arose and was directed against anything new that he might produce.

There is always resistance to any departure from established practice and it was inevitable that there would be extreme dislike of McDonnell's placing the driver in the sensible position on the left-hand side of the footplate. This change did not persist on the North Eastern after McDonnell left and over forty years elapsed before Doncaster and Darlington began to build engines with left-hand drive.

Looking ahead a little, McDonnell decided on the 4–4–0 wheel arrangement as the appropriate one for express passenger locomotives and introduced a class sometimes designated '38' which was the running number of one of those built (in 1884) at Gateshead works, and sometimes designated '1492' which was the number of one of those built (also in 1884) by Hawthorn, Leslie & Co of Newcastle.

A bogie was nothing new in North Eastern territory as Bouch had built 4–4–0s at least thirteen years earlier, but those locomotives had had unsatisfactory features and were less powerful than Fletcher's Class 901 2–4–0s that followed them. There was no bogie under any Fletcher engine for main-line passenger service (although the 'Whitby bogies' had been running for twenty years and the BTP 0–4–4Ts for ten) and so some at least of the main-line men were afraid of bogies. They expressed strong antagonism to Class 38 simply on the ground that they had bogies; the origin of this was nothing more than fear of novelty plus a modicum of unintelligence, no rare combination. It is in fact a perennial hindrance to progress and every resolute innovator is compelled to find some way of overcoming it. If he has difficulty in suffering fools gladly, or in bringing comfort to frightened children or in believing that the real reason for raising objection to anything is hardly ever the one that is offered in explanation by the objector, the end of his patience may decide him to become a dictator who gives orders without any pretence of explanation. Webb was already doing this at Crewe, and very soon T. W. Worsdell would do it at Gateshead, but McDonnell continued for some time to hope that reason might at length prevail.

In writing about the McDonnell reforms, E. L. Ahrons said that opposition of enginemen came from Newcastle and Gateshead 'Geordies'. These would form only a fraction of the staff of any department of the North Eastern Railway but nevertheless Ahrons specifically mentions them and this suggests that he had reason for discrimination. It is unlikely that many of the North Eastern's Geordies of the time were offensive; it is the low-grade mud-maker in any group that gets the group a bad name and this was probably what happened among the Geordies as seen by Ahrons. He wrote that they were radical in politics but conservative in habits and customs. This was in the *Railway Magazine* in 1917, over thirty years after the relevant events, but the usual magazine 'house style' forbade any plain description of unpleasant things and so Ahrons could do no more than hint at the truth.

One of the most interesting railway operations accessible to the lay observer on station platforms was that of 'changing enginemen' during the course of a long journey by the train. This became common in many places, especially after restriction of enginemen's working hours. Any locomotive enthusiast who shamelessly listened to what the two crews said to one another might learn a lot that has never been committed to paper. The writer has done this in many places and noted that 're-manning' on the LNER at York, normally a pleasant incident for the men concerned, could be a scene of recrimination and rancour such as was never known anywhere unless Geordies were involved. For such things as bringing a through-working engine in with hardly any fire left, or raising hell about fire, water and steam in an engine that they were re-manning, or ranting at station staff for increasing the load of a Pacific from seven vehicles to eight, Geordies were outstanding. This is not to say that more than a very few Geordies were guilty in this way, or that even the few never had any civilized moment, but in the incidents witnessed the worst offenders were exclusively Geordies.

Remembering the Ahrons account of the McDonnell trouble, one could imagine that a tradition of uncouth obstructionism had been handed down over sixty years by a line of Geordies. It may have been only a very thin line and perhaps a dotted one but its effects were easily noticeable. The individuals concerned may or may not have been radical/conservative but where they excelled was in aggressive bloodymindedness. This word had not been invented when Ahrons was writing about the obstructive Geordies and it is used now only because there seems to be no polite alternative to it.

Most people dislike change in the routine of their lives and McDonnell's prodding of North Eastern locomotive staff into states of energy probably antagonized many of them towards him. Any driver who disliked an engine could easily demonstrate that it would not do what was required of it and it was obvious that

that was how Geordie obstructionists would treat every McDonnell locomotive that came to them. There were few such engines because the rows that arose with McDonnell's campaign against the sloppiness (organizational and technical) in North Eastern motive power soon led him to appreciate that life was limited and might be tolerable if uninfested with Geordies. So he left them to it and the fact that he did so was an indictment of the general management of the North Eastern. Quite clearly it had not given McDonnell the support he deserved in the overdue job of cleaning out the Fletcherian stables. Henry Tennant, the general manager, recognized this, and that his best way of re-trieving the situation was to give himself the job of supervising the locomotive department until someone else could be persuaded to take it on. Quite clearly also, no one would do so without very firm assurance from the management that there would be no more toleration of Geordie nonsense.

For the interim period a locomotive committee was convened and chaired by Tennant. It immediately got down to the job of designing something better than the 901 Class 2–4–0s for the North Eastern main line passenger trains and it was easy to see which way to go.

Henry Tennant

During his short period of office with the North Eastern McDonnell built locomotives that looked as if they might have been designed with some regard for observers' feelings and the Tennant committee showed how easy it was in a new design to get out of the slough of ugliness that had engulfed North Eastern locomotive practice during the Fletcher period.

In designing new main-line locomotives after McDonnell had left the North Eastern, it was desirable (suggested E. L. Ahrons writing in the *Railway Magazine* in 1917) to take account of the average Geordie driver's preference to have an 'exhaust-cock' to play with and no bogie to stop him from getting at it.

The exhaust-cock was a Fletcher artifice for throwing steam away and some Geordies thought that no engine could work properly without it. It would have been unwise at that stage to make any marked departure from established North Eastern practice because a 'flop' would have been psychologically disastrous. So Tennant specified an exhaust-cock on a 2–4–0 that had to look different from a Fletcher 901. There was no difficulty in meeting these requirements and positive inspiration was to be found in some 2–4–0s built a few years earlier for the Great Northern with smoothly shaped chimneys instead of the built-up ones to which Stirling had been addicted. In this way arose the 'Tennant' 2–4–0 which also exhibited the Great Northern influence in its painted numbers instead of Fletcher brass number-plates.

Brunel once wrote: 'Now your locomotive is capable of being made very beautiful and it ought to be so.' This is well illustrated by the proximity of Fletcher No 901 and Tennant No 1463 in York Museum and detailed examination shows how little may suffice to change the crude into the elegant. The chimney is by far the most sensitive element in this respect and in the Tennant chimney appeared a combination of taper, flare-curve and rim-form that became a North Eastern hall-mark. A trace of it could be discerned even in the very short chimneys that Darlington produced for the K3 2–6–0s built there in 1924. The general form was indeed taken down to Swindon thirty years later still and used as the transverse section of double chimneys applied to 6000-class four-cylinder 4–6–0s so that (to the writer's eye looking at the front) they became changed from kings to queens.

Before any of the Tennant 2–4–0s was in service the Geordies, realising that the time for tomfoolery had passed, discovered that the McDonnell engines did in fact do all that was required of them and without exhaust-cocks. Objection to the removal of these fittings faded away and indeed one Geordie said that although he liked his engine to have an exhaust-cock he always kept it shut.

Most observers found the Tennant Class 1463 2–4–0s good to look upon and as they were rather larger than the Fletcher 901s they were better engines on the road. They had a good reputation for speed (for example a mile-a-minute York to Newcastle start to stop) and although it is not known that any of them ever approached the hottest efforts of North Western 'Precedents' they were splendid examples of the British 2-4-0.

T. W. Worsdell

Tennant must have felt very pleased when T. W. Worsdell accepted the position of locomotive superintendent of the North Eastern in 1885. Here was a man who, after a variety of jobs in his younger days, went to America at the age of 27 and within four years was in charge of the locomotive works of the Pennsylvania Railroad at Altoona. After three years there he returned to England and his next ten years he spent as works manager at Crewe and after that he was for four years locomotive superintendent of the Great Eastern Railway. A man with experience of that sort could (figuratively) eat six Geordies before breakfast and the word having seeped quickly through Gateshead, not a murmur came from the Geordies even when Worsdell pushed them into side-window cabs or when he chastised them with two-cylinder compounds.

But T. W. Worsdell's first North Eastern design was of a 2-4-2 tank engine (Class A). There was a need for a larger passenger tank engine than the Fletcher BTP 0-4-4 well-tank and as Worsdell had completed the first of a class of 2-4-2 tanks on the Great Eastern just before he left he could quickly get something similar moving in the drawing office at Gateshead. It is likely that copies of the Great Eastern drawings were sent to Gateshead; there was no reason for the Great Eastern authorities to decline to help any other railway that did not compete with them.

But even with all allowance for whatever help Worsdell may have had in this way his early work at Gateshead was rapid.

In 1886 he produced the first examples of five new designs in five different wheel-arrangements and he introduced five more classes before he retired in 1890. All these engines exhibited a sleek, discreetly decorated style that established a British standard for the ensuing forty years or more. The contrast with earlier North Eastern practice was complete although it must be added in fairness to the Fletcher ramshacklery that it did not necessarily imply functional inferiority to the better-looking locomotives that came later.

Alongside the Class A 2–4–2 tanks Worsdell produced the Class B 0–6–2 tanks closely comparable in general style and size but provided with two cylinders of different diameter for working on the principle of compound expansion. These engines were primarily for short distance goods trains and Worsdell may have had in mind that their work would provide a severe test for compounding. If it could get by in that service it would have real prospects elsewhere. To be on the safe side, or at least to provide a basis for comparison, eleven 0–6–2 tank engines (Class B1) were built with equal cylinders for simple expansion in the ordinary way, but were otherwise as Class B. Eventually the fifty one members of Class B were converted to Class B1.

As was the case on most British railways at the time, the North Eastern had a need for more goods engines. Worsdell responded to this with a two-cylinder compound 0–6–0 design and also the corresponding two-cylinder simple. In eight years 171 of the former type were built and 30 of the latter, but even this 'volume production' was only a temporary measure and four years later there appeared the first of a class of 120 larger 0–6–0s. This was the time of the great trade-boom that overtaxed Great Britain's capacity for building goods engines and led three railways to buy from America.

T. W. Worsdell's most striking mark on North Eastern locomotive design was the side-window cab he applied to all new locomotives with tenders. Such a cab was nothing new on the North Eastern; fifteen years earlier enginemen had protested against even more commodious cabs mounted by Bouch on 2/4–4–0s. But those cabs induced in the enginemen more grumbling than approbation and so Bouch gave to later engines something more like the current average North Eastern cab in the style of a sawn-off rabbit-hutch.

On the other hand, the Worsdell version of the side-window cab was accepted by enginemen without any officially recorded reluctance. It was applied to every subsequent North Eastern tender engine and it lifted the living conditions of North Eastern enginemen into the luxury class. To be able to remain warm and dry on the footplate while the engine stood in a cold, rain-laden cross-wind was something outside the most imaginative aspirations of British enginemen of the period.

It must be added that although the side-window cab was admirable in providing protection from the weather while the engine is standing or running forward it could be too hot in summer and it could be a nuisance at any time of the year when the men had to be continually looking back alongside the train as when shunting. To get his head through an opening in either side-wall, a full-sized man in the average Worsdell cab had to 'duck' and then to reverse his movements to get back to where he could make any necessary re-adjustment of the controls. This could be trying in a long spell of shunting and might be a real cause for preferring a sketchier sort of cab. On some classes of engine, at least, the side windows might usefully have been higher and indeed the Worsdell-style cabs built by Darlington Works on LNE Class K3 2–6–0s in 1924 were afterwards altered in that way. For some purposes, a single side-window in the mean position of the Worsdell twin windows might have been more convenient than they. Practice on the North British Railway suggests that this was found to be the case there.

Some North Eastern cabs, particularly those on eight-coupled engines, had so much of the boiler inside them as to make them very hot when standing and to leave uncomfortably small floor-space for firing. Even at that, they were far superior to most cabs on other British railways.

T. W. Worsdell and his North Eastern successors provided each engine with a running board immediately above buffer level and extending for the whole length of the engine. This running board height was used even where outside cylinders had to lie partly above and partly below it and even where coupling rods passed out of sight behind the running board valance in the top half of each revolution.

Besides an instinct for neatness in external design, T. W. Worsdell had an enthusiasm for compounding and a preference for Joy valve-gear. Neither of these two features won eventual wide acceptance in British practice but Worsdell is not to be criticized for pressing on with them in the 1880s.

2. No 1269 (W. Bouch) Class 238 sometimes called 'Ginx's Babies'
3. No 1809 (Fletcher) Class 492 'Whitby Bogies'
4. No 910 (Fletcher) Class 901
5. No 954 (Fletcher) Class BTP (Bogie Tank Passenger)

6. No 369 (McDonnell) *North Eastern Railway* inscribed on brass edging of splasher for main driving wheel. (Class 59)

7. No 1477 (Tennant) built at Gateshead. Marked similarity (apart from the dome) to Great Northern 2–4–0s. (Class 1463)

8. No 66 *Aerolite*. Repeatedly rebuilt tank engine in final form. (Class 66)

9. No 954 (Class 290). Nominal rebuild of Fletcher BTP

Rational examination of the physics of compounding in steam locomotives would have shown however that its possible advantage was hardly big enough to be discernible with certainty in normal service conditions.

The advantage of Joy valve-gear in working valves above the cylinders and in not cluttering the crank-axle with eccentrics was so great that it justified thorough trial in service. The outcome was, as we know now, but could not have foreseen in 1886, that Joy gear was used on the North Western and on the Lancashire & Yorkshire to the almost complete exclusion of other types of valve-gear for as long as those railways continued to build locomotives, but that no other railway used it extensively or for very long.

A characteristic of T. W. Worsdell's four coupled tender-engines was the enclosure of the parts of each pair of the driving wheels that protruded above the running board in a single splasher spread out nearly to the maximum permissible width of the engine. Each splasher was edged with a brass strip in the form of two quadrant arcs and a straight line. This strip drew attention to large but functionally insignificant parts of the locomotive and the writer found it less attractive than the use in Class R of two semi-circular strips paralleling the wheel rims.

T. W. Worsdell enclosed Ramsbottom-type safety-valves in a neat brass casing and this characterized all new North Eastern locomotives till 'pop' safety-valves started to become popular in Britain about 1911. Before that time the larger North Eastern engines had Ramsbottom safety-valves in duplicate and their brass casing perforce took a form that was gross rather than elegant.

T. W. Worsdell early applied the two-cylinder compound principle in 0–6–0s, 2–4–0s and 4–4–0s (Classes C, D and F) and this was natural enough. It was surprising that he should also use it in 0–6–2 tank engines (Class B) as these were for short distance goods service that inevitably included a lot of starting from rest, the operation at which compound engines were at their worst. Of Classes I and J it may be said that if it were deemed worthwhile in 1888 to build 'single-drivers' (and certainly some other

C

33

British railways built such engines as many as thirteen years later) they might as well be compounds if compounding was in favour on the railway concerned at the time.

The Class I 4–2–2s were straightforward elegant-looking engines with no unusual design-feature anywhere. They were intended for the normally light trains running between Leeds, York and Scarborough and it was recognized that something more powerful was necessary for the heaviest North Eastern trains on the East Coast main line. But the designer of that similar but larger engine ran immediately into difficult circumstances of the kind that prohibits a pint-pot from containing a quart of water. In a locomotive the cylinder-block was normally placed between the frame-plates which lay between the wheel flanges which lay between the rail-heads which were separated by 4 ft 8½ in. In consequence the width of the cylinder-block had to be limited to about 4 ft.

In the larger 4–2–2s (Class J) this was not enough and so the cylinders were disposed rather unconventionally and the steam-chests were outside the frame.

Wilson Worsdell

When T. W. Worsdell retired from the North Eastern in 1890, his place was taken by his brother Wilson Worsdell who was already on the North Eastern, and had indeed joined its locomotive department some two years before T. W. Worsdell came from the Great Eastern.

The first new design to materialize after Wilson Worsdell's accession was the numerically small but physically large Class L 0–6–0T. It was the largest North Eastern locomotive of this wheel arrangement and only ten were built whereas other very similar designs ran to anything up to 120 in a class.

Wilson Worsdell had seen too much of compounding to like it; he also saw that 'single-drivers' were not going to be of much use for the heavier main line trains that the North Eastern expected to be running in the future. So his first design for such service was the Class M1 4–4–0, helped to look massive by an extended smokebox.

'Extended' here means made longer than the diameter of the mounting flange of the chimney. In many contemporary British locomotives the smokebox had been made as short as possible and flat-chestedness was common. This is not so eyeable as a little prominence, and extension of the smokebox even for a few inches ahead of the chimney-base can transform the appearance of a locomotive.

Class M1 had steam-chests outside the frame-plates. This was not because there was any difficulty in finding room for them inside the frame but probably because Worsdell had seen some advantage, demonstrated in Class J, in the ready accessibility of valves in that position.

Motion had to be applied to the valves from the Stephenson valve-gear by rocking shafts but, apart from the extra parts, there was nothing very bad about this. Compared with what T. W. Worsdell had done on Class J 4–2–2s the mechanism of Class M1 was elegant.

Nevertheless the outside steam chests went out of North Eastern favour. The original Class M1 cylinders were replaced by conventional inside cylinders and when this was done the extended smokebox also disappeared. The first engine to be changed was No 1623 in 1903.

Perhaps as a sop to his brother who as a consultant still retained a connection with the North Eastern, Wilson Worsdell built one engine (No 1619) of what was virtually Class M1 as a two-cylinder compound.

But by 1894 T. W. Worsdell had relinquished his connection with the North Eastern and Wilson Worsdell at once began to rebuild the two-cylinder compound engines as ordinary two-cylinder 'simples' and to replace Joy valve-gear by link-motion. But not everyone on the North Eastern was anti-compound. Someone—probably W. M. Smith, the Chief Draughtsman—persuaded Worsdell to have No 1619 rebuilt in 1898 to become a three-cylinder compound. This was more complicated than before but it was at least symmetrical in its cylinder-arrangement. Wilson Worsdell was evidently persuaded to try at least one such engine but could not be dissuaded from scrapping two-cylinder compounds and Joy valve-gear.

Over on the North Western at Crewe an analogous position arose a few years later where after the retirement of Webb, George Whale proceeded to scrap the three-cylinder compounds as fast as two-cylinder 4–4–0s could be built to replace them but he retained Joy valve-gear even in new construction as indeed did his successors at Crewe.

A Worsdell practice that seemed to the writer to be rather playful was to put the Westinghouse pump well inside the big splasher with the wheels so that only the tip of the steam-valve casing could be seen. Abreast of the pump, the elliptical brass number-plate hung on a hinge and could be swung upwards to expose a good deal of the cylinder-and-pump assembly.

Separate splashers would have left the pump much more conveniently exposed for attention and would have permitted the men to loosen up a 'sticking' steam valve by throwing coal at it without leaving the footplate. Much use was made of this dodge on some parts of the LNER during World War II and after it.

Wilson Worsdell kept the North Eastern in step with the other British railways in the 'five foot six'-boiler phase that occurred in the early years of the twentieth century and the North Eastern 'big engines' looked as large and neat as any. But before that stage he had covered the 'bread and butter' needs of the company in tank engines for goods and passenger work and in 0–6–0s for goods and mineral traffic.

His 0–6–2Ts of Class N of 1894 were very similar to his brother's Class B1 of 1886, but he made no addition to the 60 Class A 2–4–2Ts. Instead the Class O 0–4–4T was introduced in 1894 and 110 of them were built in the succeeding ten years. This change in policy (in a sense a reversion to Fletcher) is interesting as a symmetrical ('double-end') wheel arrangement might naturally be thought to be advantageous in a locomotive that had to cover equal mileage in both directions and had, moreover, to run quite fast with many of its passenger trains. For this class of service the Lancashire & Yorkshire used exclusively 2–4–2Ts with Joy valve-gear, whereas Wilson Worsdell pointedly rejected such construction in favour of 0–4–4Ts with link motion. This merely emphasizes that almost any locomotive design problem could be solved equally well in several different ways.

Although Class M1 4-4-0s Nos 1620 and 1621 had distinguished themselves by fast running in the 1895 Race to Scotland, Worsdell, even so early in the career of this class, had fallen out of love with the outside steam chests and, wanting more 4-4-0s in 1896, produced Class Q which differed from Class M1 in little more than the use of link motion, connected through rocking-shafts to flat valves above the cylinders. Three years later he used in the slightly larger Class R 4-4-0, link-motion with direct drive to piston valves underneath the cylinders. This may seem to be a queer place for valves, but Class R turned out to be the best 4-4-0 on the North Eastern and the same construction was used in many of the double-frame 4-4-0s on the Great Western Railway.

But a more striking North Eastern step in 1899 was its entry into the 'outside-cylinder' big engine class by the production of the Class S 2/4-6-0. As so often happened on British railways the result of thus breaking new ground was not brilliant (although forty of Class S were built) but it would not have been rational to assume that it was the change from inside cylinders to outside cylinders that had introduced a dubious element in the design. Certainly there was nothing to criticize in the result of employing outside cylinders in the 200-odd North Eastern eight-coupled goods engines the first of which appeared in 1901.

Wilson Worsdell had spent some years in America, and was a friend of G. J. Churchward who was much influenced by American practice in developing Great Western standard designs from 1902. Nevertheless North Eastern designs showed no American characteristic; its side-window cab certainly looked like one but Bouch had introduced it in North Eastern territory as far back as 1860. On the contrary, Worsdell adhered to the British Victorian tradition of using a low running board and hiding things rather than exposing them. Worsdell did his best to hide outside cylinders and mechanism by keeping the running board right down at buffer-beam level and this made big North Eastern engines look top-heavy, while flat smokeboxes did not improve their appearance.

Perhaps the most noticeable locomotives in this respect were the 0–6–0s of Classes P2 and P3. Here the smokebox was bigger in diameter even than the lagging plates on a 5 ft 6 in boiler and was only just wide enough to carry the chimney. By comparison with the average British 0–6–0 in 1904 the P2s looked enormous and some members of the enginemens' union tried to stir up trouble by asserting that these engines were dangerously top-heavy. That suggestion found no confirmation in the long history of Classes P2 and P3 and indeed it now seems maliciously imaginative in view of experience with hundreds of LNE J38 and J39 0–6–0s with much more highly-pitched boilers.

Against the 155 large 0–6–0s, the 90 0–8–0s and the 60 Class R 4–4–0s, the 20 'Atlantics' of Worsdell design may seem hardly worth mentioning and indeed their work, as seen by locomotive enthusiasts, was never outstanding in relation to their size. They were much better than the 4–6–0s because they were bigger in the firebox and in ash-pan clearances. In 1903 their short chimneys impressed amateur observers who were consequently inclined to believe the suggestion that they were the biggest engines that could be built within the British loading gauge, but the illusion did not survive the appearance of Swindon's 'Great Bear' Pacific in 1908.

Worsdell allowed W. M. Smith to 'twist his arm' sufficiently to make him agree to the building of a couple of four-cylinder compound Atlantics of which the most notable feature was the deep valance extending over the length of the engine between a raised running board and a line at buffer-beam height. Unique on the North Eastern was the Belpaire firebox on each engine and inside Walschaerts valve-gear on one of them.

A strange story about these engines is that W. M. Smith had taken out a patent on some feature in their design and that after his death, building of a considerable number of similar ones was stopped by a demand for high royalty payments by the executors of the patentee. What makes this hard to believe is the fact that any patent taken out by a designer in respect of a development within the scope of his employment, is automatically the property of his employer.

Inspiration from outside the North Eastern led Worsdell to a development that spread on that system and characterized the design of large locomotives on the LNER. This was the use of three cylinders in a non-compound locomotive. Robinson did this in his 0-8-4T shunters built in 1908 for the hump-shunting yard at Wath-on-Dearne. In 1909 for similar service in the Erimus yard near Middlesbrough Worsdell built Class X three-cylinder 4-8-0 tank engines. In the following year appeared Class Y three-cylinder 4-6-2 tank engines and Raven used three cylinders in Atlantics and 4-4-4Ts built in 1911 and 1913.

Vincent L Raven

World War I started so soon after Raven's promotion to the top job in North Eastern steam that he had neither need nor opportunity for any extensive development of locomotives for express passenger service. He did in fact make only one step in that direction, but it was a notable one.

Wilson Worsdell's Class V 'Atlantics' were adequate and his Class VI engines were perhaps slightly better, but left something to be desired. Raven had been rather impressed by the three-cylinder principle and it seemed worth trying in an 'Atlantic'. So he fitted three cylinders instead of four into the general layout of Class 4CC, used the Worsdell 'Atlantic' boiler, to feed steam directly to all three cylinders, and thus gave the North Eastern its best big passenger engine, the majestic Class Z.

Raven's next design, the 3/4-4-4T of Class D was not perhaps the best possible one for the jobs it normally did, nor were those jobs the easiest ones for an outside observer to assess. He went on to apply three cylinders in enlarged versions of North Eastern 4-6-0 and 0-8-0 designs and also in much bigger engines, the North Eastern 'Pacifics'.

But none of these surpassed the excellence of Class Z which was a consummation of the Edwardian steam locomotive and the North Eastern's finest weight-pulling 'flyer'.

CHAPTER 3

SIX-COUPLED SIX-WHEELERS

EXAMINATION of Table 5 shows that nearly 400 0–6–0s were built for the North Eastern between 1872 and 1886 and well over 500 between 1886 and 1923; over 700 of them were surviving at the end of December 1922 in a North Eastern total of about 2100 locomotives.

This proportion was representative of British railways and emphasizes that goods traffic provided the 'bread and butter'. The make-up of goods trains, their haulage and their subsequent division were not, in the ordinary way, dramatic operations for either the operator or the observer and there was no easy means of judging how well a goods engine was working. Hard slogging with a big load up a gradient produced a very satisfying noise for the enthusiast, but it did not necessarily mean that the engine was developing high power. Figures for pounds of coal per mile were obtainable for individual locomotives, but in the unavoidable absence of quantitative information about the amount of work done in running the miles, those figures had no technical meaning. So it must be accepted that there is no reliable means of assessing the relative merits of North Eastern goods engines or of comparing their work with that of corresponding locomotives on other railways.

Goods engines commonly lasted for forty to fifty years and there were several contributory reasons for such longevity. The mileage per year was not usually high, the power developed was low, even when pulling hard because the speed was low and, also for that reason, it was not necessary to keep the engines in tip-top mechanical condition. But any breakdown of an engine on a main line might paralyze half the railway system. So no goods engine (nor any other) that might have to go on to a main line could be allowed to get so bad as to suffer undue risk of breakdown.

That the power demanded of goods engines did not change very rapidly with the years is suggested by the fact that after the building of the first Class 398 0–6–0 in 1872, thirty-two years elapsed before the North Eastern had any larger 0–6–0. During that period, 770 0–6–0s were added to the company's stock; increase in goods traffic was met by more numerous locomotives rather than by larger locomotives.

By the end of the nineteenth century, requirements evidently changed, as 0–8–0s began to appear on the North Eastern in 1901, but there was still scope for big 0–6–0s and fifty were built in 1904–05, followed by a hundred or so between 1906 and 1923. On sheer numbers, the 0–6–0 must be judged to be the most important type of locomotive in North Eastern history.

0–6–0 Tender engines
Class 1001
Class 1001 did not represent the typical 0–6–0 as its firebox was behind the rear axle. The engine was made on the Stephenson 'long-boiler' plan which had the advantage of minimizing the wheel-base for a given length of boiler. The value of this lay in the ability of the engine to pass round very sharp curves such as those to be found in many colliery sidings. It could not do this at any considerable speed nor was it in fact safe at speed even on straight track. This was because the overhang of the cylinders ahead of the wheels and that of the firebox behind the wheels invited oscillation ('sway') about a central vertical axis, and also oscillation ('porpoising') about a central transverse axis. Class 1001 was no 'flyer' but it was fast enough for short-distance goods and mineral traffic. The need to keep its rear overhang within reasonable limits restricted the size of the firebox and therefore the sustained power output. One can, in imagination, see it at work as a six-wheeled slender sausage with a little firebox and a couple of men clinging on to the back as best they could. There

was nothing to prevent a sideways lurch (and there must have been plenty of them) from throwing the firemen off balance and indeed off the engine, through the 3 ft wide gap between the tender and what one might, in an unguarded moment, refer to as the 'cab'.

The 'long-boiler' concept led to an engine that was very uncomfortable for its crew and one feels that the men must have hated Class 1001. On the other hand, when one remembers enginemen's rejection of Bouch's large side-window cab on his earliest 2/4–4–40s, one is inclined to believe that inurement to bad conditions leads to toleration of them (and even to affection for them) and so to hostility to any suggestion for improvement. One hates to think of enginemen being pelted by cold, gale-blown rain because their engine provided no shelter for them, where there was plenty of power to cope with the weight and windage of a really protective cab.

No record has come down to us of any Class 1001 engine touching seventy miles an hour, or even forty. They puffed about very cautiously with loose-coupled and even dumb-buffered coal wagons, not trying very hard to keep time if indeed any precise timetables were ever prepared for North Eastern coal-trains when Class 1001 was in its prime.

One of the novelties of nationalization in Durham was a system whereby the enginemen and guards allotted to the job of getting the day's output of particular collieries to the appropriate marshalling yard were paid a particular sum of money for it and they could go home when they had done it. This revealed unsuspected power and speed in engines and men, and it was perhaps well for Class 1001 engines that they never had to participate in frolics of this kind.

As it was, they lasted very well and once past the end of the Fletcher period, they saw better days to the extent that they received boilers with reasonable-looking chimneys and eyeable domes instead of the atrocities they originally bore.

Class 1001 had the usual Fletcher range of variations in detail. The dimensions quoted for it in Table 5 have wider ranges of uncertainty than those for locomotives with less casual backgrounds. The figures are intended to convey an impression of the size of the engine and in view of all the circumstances, that is about as much as can reasonably be expected.

Class 1001 has a survivor (No 1275) in York Museum. It stands next to a Fletcher 2-4-0, No 910, with a Tennant 2-4-0 and a Worsdell 4-4-0 on the next track. It helps to demonstrate that the North Eastern did make some progress in locomotive design in the nineteenth century.

Class 398

When T. W. Worsdell took charge of North Eastern locomotive matters in 1885 he proceeded to get out some new designs and he gave to each of them a class-letter. It was hardly possible to do this for existing classes as they were far too numerous to be contained in any single alphabet or indeed in any logical system of designation. Any attempt that may have been made to do so in respect of 0-6-0s was abandoned. A group of 325 of them were bunched together as Class 398 even though they had such variations as four different wheel-diameters ranging from 4 ft 9 in to 5 ft 8 in. Over a period of nine years they had been built by the North Eastern at Darlington, Gateshead and York and by at least five 'outside' firms.

The Class 398 engines were all conventional single-frame 0-6-0s with firebox and cylinders in the usual places, but apart from that there was endless variety in them. The dimension quoted in Table 5 for Class 398 may be taken as representative averages; it is improbable that they are all correct for any particular engine.

Following some explosions of boilers on Class 398s and of similar boilers on other engines, re-boilering of Class 398 was begun much earlier than was usual. Locomotive boilers commonly lasted for twenty years, but re-boilering of Class 398s began after less than seven years. Boiler explosions continued, however, until as late as 1888. These were obviously the most dramatic incidents in the long career of Class 398 but they attract attention only because locomotive boiler explosions have been mercifully rare in Great Britain. Not every other country has nearly so creditable a record in this respect.

In their early years Class 398 naturally worked the main-line goods trains and, equally naturally, they were relegated to lighter goods work when bigger goods engines eventually became numerous on the North Eastern.

With the gay irresponsibility that was a surprising feature here and there in Victorian railway philosophy, the early members of Class 398 were let loose with no brakes. Retardation had to be effected by a hand-brake on the tender or by reversing the engine with regulator open. The first advance from this primitive state was to fit the engine with hand-brakes worked by a handle on a column that was an obstructive nuisance to the fireman. The next step was to fit steam brakes and, in the 1880s, Westinghouse pumps began to be applied to some engines so that they might work passenger trains. Later on, the compressed air was used to apply brakes on the engine itself. Some of the class indeed were 'dual-fitted' for working either Westinghouse brakes or vacuum brakes. These provisions for using Class 398 engines or passenger trains were, in general, limited to those with 5 ft or 5 ft 8 in wheels; they were made as a means of providing motive power for 'extra' passenger trains such as 'excursions' or 'race specials' rather than for regular passenger trains.

Although hundreds of 0-6-0s were added to North Eastern stock after Class 398 was complete, it continued in service for a long time. Eighty engines of the class survived till 1923 and the last was withdrawn from service in 1928.

Class 59

The 0-6-0s produced by McDonnell in 1883-85 with wavy running boards immediately called to mind Webb's 'Cauliflower' 18 in 0-6-0s on the North Western. A noticeable difference was that while the 'Cauliflower' had three waves on each side, Class 59 showed variations. The cab side-sheets were set near enough to the edge of the running board to form splashers that accommodated the rear wheels and the rear ends of the coupling rods, without any necessity for a third wave. You had to see both sides of an engine before deciding what entry to make in your records under the heading 'Number of waves'.

The cab bore some resemblance to the 'Cauliflower' cab—if it could be called a cab—and was perhaps not so commodious as some of the cabs on Class 398 engines. Crewe practice was followed in the use of screw reversing gear on the left side of the engine and in the use of Ramsbottom-type safety-valves.

These engines were larger than some 0–6–0s that McDonnell had built for the Great Southern & Western, but not quite so large as the average Class 398 0–6–0. So there may have been some substance in the complaint that Class 59 engines were less powerful than Class 398. After McDonnell had left the North Eastern, however, drivers applied to have Class 59 engines allotted to them and this confirmed the suspicion that earlier criticism was just a bit of exhaust-cock Geordiness.

Classes C and C1

Every locomotive-shed foreman liked to have engines that could take either passenger trains or goods trains with reasonable efficiency and, at least before World War I, British practice was to build 0–6–0s with this in view. It was always safe to produce some more 0–6–0s and T. W. Worsdell was not long in getting round to it. Within a year or so of his taking charge of North Eastern steam he had turned out the first of his Class C1 0–6–0s and also the first of his Class C 0–6–0s which were two-cylinder compounds. Ten of the former appeared in 1886; twenty more followed in 1894–5. In the intervening period, however, 171 compound engines of Class C were built and in 1889 T. W. Worsdell reported that, with boiler steam at 160 lb per sq in, they burned 14 per cent less coal than the corresponding 'simples' with boiler steam at 140 lb per sq in. It is not certain than anyone believed that economy of that order could be achieved by all the engines of the class in regular service. Nor is it known that coal-saving to this extent was regularly effected by compounding, but in 1894 the North Eastern Locomotive Committee reported in favour of converting Class C compounds to 'simples' as they came out of service for heavy repair. This was done, but it was not

45

until 1913 that the last engine was converted to Class C1 which was then re-lettered Class C presumably to keep historians on their toes.

The earlier converted engines had flat valves and Joy valve-gear as in the original Class C1 but later conversions were to a modified Class C1 with link-motion working piston-valves below the cylinders.

Superheaters began to be applied to the new Class C in 1914 but engines began to be withdrawn from service before super-heating had caught up with them. Moreover, superheaters were removed from some engines and there were never at any one time more than about a third of the total number of Class C 0–6–0s with superheaters. It looks as if the authorities were as doubtful of the value of superheating as their predecessors had been about compounding.

Most of the original Class C engines had steam brakes and were not fitted for working passenger trains, but over the years Westinghouse brake equipment, vacuum brake equipment and steam heating pipes were added to many of Classes C and C1. They were used for a wide variety of duties all over the North Eastern system. They were for a long time the regular passenger train engines for the bleak severity of Stainmore summit; at the other extreme they could take 700 tons at an average of 20 mph on the level lines from Gascoigne Wood to Hull or Thirsk. With a passenger train of a few coaches they could run at a mile a minute on the flat.

Classes P P1 P2 and P3
By the year 1894, the recurrent demand for more 0–6–0s turned up again and to meet it Wilson Worsdell produced Class P, very similar to Class C1 but slightly smaller and lighter. This is at first sight surprising but perhaps more so was the next move which was to produce in 1898 Class P1 whose dimensions placed it within the small gap between Classes C and P. Failure to find, or to imagine, any rational explanation for the piffling differences between these classes suggests that the demon of anti-standardiza-tion, against which Fletcher was powerless, had not been com-

pletely exorcized even by the down-to-earth Worsdells, and made occasional return visits to Gateshead.

The next size of 0–6–0, Class P2, produced in 1904, looked different because it had a 5 ft 6 in boiler, the fattest fitted to a British 0–6–0 at that time. It provided more weight to grip the rails and so the P2 really was a stronger puller. Its smokebox was distinctly bigger than the lagged boiler barrel and the engine looked rather 'pot-bellied', top-heavy and not very stable. None of these things had any operational significance and the engines safely coped well with heavy mineral trains at the highest speeds that were prudent with such trains.

The P2 boiler had a sloping grate lying partly over the rear axle. The grate area was some 18 per cent greater than that of Class P1, which only slightly exceeded the 17 sq ft of Class 398, originated in 1872.

Class P3 differed from Class P2 only in the slope of the firegrate and the depth of the firebox.

These larger 0–6–0s were purely goods engines with steam brakes, three-link couplings and no provision for working passenger trains. Like the other North Eastern 0–6–0s they were fitted with superheaters only after about 1913 if at all, but many of them were changed back to become 'wet steam' engines. This was probably done because many of their duties were made up of pulling-spells too short for the fire to warm up enough to give the superheater any perceptible value.

Superheating was applied in North Eastern 0–6–0s only to engines with piston-valves.

0–6–0 Tank engines

Among tank engines the 0–6–0 wheel arrangement was as 'popular' as it was for tender engines. In each of the two groups there were far more 0–6–0s than there were locomotives of any other wheel arrangement. But on most railways 0–6–0 tank engines did not normally haul passenger trains and so the student of the locomotive had little chance to become enthusiastic over the ability of 0–6–0Ts to make sparkling runs for him to time. Certainly that did not happen on the North Eastern and its 0–6–0 tank engines were used as shunters in passenger stations and in goods yards, and as motive agents for short-distance goods trains. The relative virtues of different classes of o–6–oT were not based on dimensions of boiler or cylinders but rather on convenience of controls for braking and quick reversal, convenience in taking on water and coal, convenience in getting rid of dusty cinder and ash from smokebox and ash-pan, and convenience in coping with running repairs. These are qualities that can be assessed only by actual experience and there can never have been many people who could compare North Eastern engines with (say) Great Western engines in such respects as these. If asked whether this or that North Eastern o–6–oT was generally superior to this or that o–6–oT of any other railway we have to say that we do not know.

The North Eastern Class 290 o–6–oT was interesting in that it was said to be a 'rebuild' of the Fletcher BTP o–4–4T. Acceptance of this demands a very loose interpretation of the word 'rebuild' but boiler, cylinders, motion and crank-axle may have been transferred from one engine to another in some cases. Class 290 lived long and fewer than a dozen of them had been withdrawn from service by the end of 1935.

The most numerous o–6–oTs were those of Class E (LNE J71) normally limited to goods service as they lacked, in general, apparatus for working either Westinghouse brakes or vacuum brakes.

Next in total number came Class E1 (LNE J72) of which seventy-five were built by the North Eastern between 1898 and 1921. Ten were added by the LNER in 1925 and fifteen more by British Railways in 1949. This seems to indicate that Class E1 was regarded by BR engineers as being among the best of the very numerous o–6–oTs produced by the railways of Britain over about seventy years.

The heaviest of the o–6–oTs was Class L, of which ten were built in 1891–2 and no further addition was ever made to the class.

Class H1 (o–6–o CT) was an extension of the Class H o–4–oT. On the extended frame where the bunker would normally have

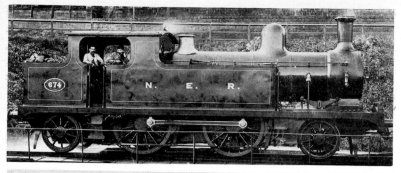

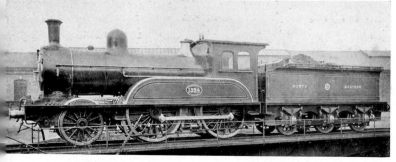

0. No 674 (Class A) on turntable at Whitby. Even the chimney is bright
1. No 855 (Class B). A goods traffic adaptation of Class A
2. No 871 (Class C). Joy valve-gear. Double side-window cab
3. No 1324 (Class D). Two-cylinder compound with Joy valve-gear

14. No 2143 (Class D of 1913). Note Westinghouse pump, steam-reverser mechanical lubricator. Pop safety valves. No 2143 composed of same figures as for original Class D.

15. No 299 (Class E). Larger-wheel version of Class 290. Deep buffer beams.

16. No 115 (Class F). Driver feeling important. Fireman not putting on airs for anybody.

17. No 676 (Class G). Note Joy valve-gear and flat valves. Driver showing shirt-sleeves in homely cab.

been placed was mounted a steam-driven swivelling jib-crane. To take the weight of this crane and whatever it lifted, an extra pair of coupled wheels were added to the two pairs in Class H.

When the crane was centred for travelling, its hook hung over the centre of the boiler just where the dome would normally have been. There was still room for a dome on the first ring of the boiler but none was provided. Perhaps it was desired that the engine should be able to travel with a load hanging on the crane hook; the space between the chimney and the safety-valve admitted a load about 6 feet long. Or perhaps it was realised that carefree slewing of the crane could cause the hook to hit any dome on the boiler. The chimney would have to take its chance.

Class H2 was substantially the same as Class H1 except that it had a bunker instead of a crane. There was nothing to prohibit the mounting of a dome on its boiler, but the value of interchangeability of boilers between Classes H1 and H2 outweighed any disadvantage of domelessness.

CHAPTER 4

NOTES ON THE VARIOUS CLASSES

Class 901 (*2–4–0*)

THE best-known of the Fletcher engines were probably the 2–4–0s of Class 901. By 'best-known' is meant the class that North Eastern historians invariably mention in connection with McDonnell, exhaust-cocks, Geordies and the 'trouble'. Fifty-five of them had been built over a period of ten years, the last of them not long before Fletcher retired and they were running all the 'best' North Eastern passenger trains when McDonnell took charge of North Eastern steam. So when he included among his innovations, removal of exhaust-cocks from Class 901, he achieved in Geordie eyes the limit of impious desecration. It was the most dramatic incident in the whole career of the 901s before T. W. Worsdell began to rebuild them.

The Fletcher exhaust-cock was in effect a variable blast-pipe and every driver was glad to have it as a means of coping with bad steaming by simply pulling a lever. It is easy to understand therefore that McDonnell's removal of this established stand-by would perturb enginemen for a time at least.

Nineteen 901s were built at Gateshead between 1872 and 1870 and sixteen more between 1880 and 1882. In the interim, Beyer-Peacock and Neilson each supplied ten of these engines. There were many variations in detail and perhaps the most significant comment on the operational value of the 901s is that nearly all of them were rebuilt before 1888.

Each 901 began with a Salter safety-valve on the dome, which at this distance in time suggests a Midland engine, and a stove-pipe chimney which suggests Great Eastern, but the gaudy lining-out, faithfully reproduced in most line-drawings of the engines, could only be North Eastern. The second safety-valve was of the Naylor type not (in the early Gateshead and Beyer-Peacock engines) on the seating on the firebox, but between the dome and the chimney. Neilsons, however, placed the safety-valve in the usual position and Gateshead followed suit in the 1880–2 batch of sixteen. Wooden brake-blocks were used at first, but by 1880 or so, the usual cast-iron blocks had replaced them.

Reversing and cut-off adjustment were effected by a tall lever with the usual latch, but a long horizontal screw was also provided, and a nut on it had a rotatable block that could be set to bear against the reversing lever. So the screw could be used to move the lever over short distances and the block could be set to prevent the lever from moving in one direction or the other, but not both at the same time.

McDonnell was with the North Eastern for only a short time, but he had to do something about the 901s. No engineer brought up elsewhere and noting (for example) the austere dignity of the early Webb locomotives, could calmly accept the vulgarity of the looks of the North Eastern engines and, as a start, McDonnell altered No 362 so as to make it look more like a North Western 'Jumbo'. The Salter safety-valve was removed, the Naylor valve replaced by one of the Ramsbottom-type, and dark green colour, with restrained fine lining substituted for the Fletcher fairground painting.

A change that must have infuriated the Geordies was removal of the Fletcher reversing gear in favour of plain screw-reverse on the left side of the engine instead of the right. With station-platforms and signals on the left, this change in the position of the driver made for safety, but it threatened firemen with the need to fire left-handed, as there was not much space between the wheel-splashers in the cab of a 2–4–0. (On the North Western however, right-hand firing was normal.)

The Tennant 2–4–0s, built after McDonnell had left the North Eastern, gave T. W. Worsdell inspiration for further rebuilding of the 901s and he made them look presentable. Later still one of them, No 167, was rebuilt by Wilson Worsdell with a distinctly larger boiler to become perhaps the most impressive 2–4–0 ever to run in Britain. The Great Eastern 'Humpty-Dumpty' 2–4–0s were comparable, but looked just a shade awkward. This, no doubt, was what gave rise to their nickname.

Class BTP (0–4–4WT)

The tank engines built for the North Eastern during Edward Fletcher's thirty years of superintendence were perhaps the most notable of the locomotives designed under his supervision. They included the 'Bogie Tank Passenger' engines which were well-tank engines with 0–4–4 wheel arrangement. Some 120 of these were built in five different works between 1874 and 1883. Forty-odd of them became LNER engines in 1923, but all had been withdrawn by 1930.

As usual with Fletcher designs these engines had innumerable variations in detail but that did not prevent them from doing very good work for their size in almost every short-distance passenger train service on the North Eastern.

The introduction of the Class A 2–4–2Ts from 1886 and the Class O 0–4–4Ts from 1894 naturally took away from the BTPs much of their heavier work and so from 1899 they began to be withdrawn from service. Boilers that were still serviceable for some time ahead were used in sixty Class 290 0–6–0Ts built between 1898 and 1922.

From 1905 a number of the BTPs were adapted to work 'push and pull' with a coach or coaches on services in County Durham and, for example, from Hull, York, Leeds and Harrogate. Such trains were light and well within the capacity of the BTPs which were, for the 1900s, quite small engines. Even smaller ones were in the steam 'rail-cars' provided by the LNER in the late 1920s for some of the very lightest passenger services in various parts of the ex-North Eastern system.

Well-tank engines in Britain were few compared with side-tank engines. It may be useful to add that a well-tank engine is one in which the water is carried in a tank situated under the coal in the bunker. The capacity of such a tank is much less than that of the side-tanks that might be carried in the usual position, and so the engine is limited to short runs between water cranes and/ or to easy running conditions.

Class A   (2-4-2T)

T. W. Worsdell's first North Eastern design was a 2-4-2T slightly larger than the very similar one that he had produced as Class M15 (LNE F4) on the Great Eastern Railway, two years earlier. It showed that the purification of appearance, begun at Gateshead by McDonnell and extended in the Tennant 2-4-0s, had taken a big step further. It demonstrated a neat functionalism that was characteristic of nearly all subsequent British 2-4-2Ts; they showed remarkably little variation in layout and dimensions. Only the Lancashire & Yorkshire Railway perpetuated else-where, in such engines, Worsdell's use of Joy valve-gear. The mechanism has been suspected (probably without evidence) of being responsible for heavy coal consumption by Worsdell's Great Eastern 2-4-2Ts of which it has been said (in print) that, 'the class always rejoiced in the name of *Worsdell Gobblers*'. Whatever may have been the intended significance of that hideous name, it is hard to imagine why it should cause rejoicing.

Absence of exhaust-cocks from Class A cannot have endeared it to the Geordies, but if they did think up some nasty name for the class no one has seen fit to put it into print.

The building of sixty Class A locomotives in six years shows that they gave early satisfaction, and the survival of all of them till 1928 and the last of them till 1938 shows that they continued to give useful service for a long time.

So also did Wilson Worsdell's Class O 0-4-4Ts which had boilers and cylinders identical with those of Class A. The successful operation of these two classes and of tank engines of these wheel arrangements on other British railways gives no hint that either had any marked superiority over the other.

Classes B B1 N U   (0-6-2T)

T. W. Worsdell's first compound engines for the North Eastern were the Class B 0–6–2 tank engine and its counterpart the Class C 0–6–0 tender engine.

Compound engines in general were not good at starting from rest and two-cylinder compounds do not exhibit compounding at its best in this respect. So to apply the system to a 'goods' tank engine which had naturally to do a lot of starting and stopping seemed rather odd. Nevertheless fifty-one such engines were built between 1886 and 1890 and during the same period eleven counterpart 'simple' engines (Class B1) were also produced. These formed the pattern for rebuilding Class B engines as soon as Wilson Worsdell could decently get his hands on them. They had Joy valve-gear as built and as first rebuilt but, when cylinders wore beyond re-boring, new ones were substituted with under-slung piston valves worked by Stephenson gear.

Class N, of which there were twenty engines built in 1893–4, differed from Class B1 in having a 26 in piston-stroke instead of 24 and in having link-motion working valves above the cylinders through rocking shafts.

Class U (twenty engines built 1902–3) differed from Class N in having cylinders $\frac{1}{2}$ in smaller in diameter, and driving wheels 6 inches smaller in diameter. Link motion worked piston valves below the cylinders. All these engines were employed mostly, but not exclusively, in goods train service, and they survived till well after the grouping of 1923.

1886 Class D (2–4–0)

In 1886, T. W. Worsdell built a two-cylinder compound 2–4–0 No 1324 with 6 ft 8 in wheels and Joy valve-gear that worked flat valves above the cylinders.

Two years later there appeared No 340, a generally similar locomotive but having a piston-valve for the high-pressure cylinder and two smaller piston-valves for the low-pressure cylinder. The valves were described as 'Smith's patent' but they were unlikely to have been of the same design as Smith's 'seg-mental' piston-valves fitted over ten years later to M1 class 4–4–0s.

In No 340 the H.P. valve was $7\frac{1}{2}$ inches in diameter, which was appropriate for an 18 in cylinder, but even *two* 5½ in valves were hardly enough for a 26 in cylinder.

Perhaps the best comment that may be made about these engines is to remark that no other engine similar to either of them was ever built and that they themselves were rebuilt as ordinary 4–4–0s with two inside cylinders and became members of Class F1.

Classes F and F1 (4–4–0)

Between 1887 and 1891, the North Eastern built twenty-five two-cylinder compound 4–4–0s, substantially like No 1324 except for the use of leading bogies. They were designated Class F.

It is hard to find any reason why these engines might do better work on fast trains than did the 'Tennant' 2–4–0s and there seems to be no evidence that they did. The leading bogie of an F might make it a better-riding engine than a 'Tennant' and indeed the conversion of the Class D 2–4–0s Nos 1324 and 340 to the 4–4–0 wheel-arrangement suggests that the heavy cylinder-block was found to be a bit too much to mount ahead of the leading axle.

Class F did not distinguish itself in general service, and even the claim that in the 1888 'Race to Scotland' No 117 averaged slightly over 60 mph with 100 tons from Newcastle to Edinburgh is seen to be mild when compared with the 67.2 mph averaged by North Western *Hardwicke* with 80 tons from Crewe to Carlisle in 1895. Even after it had been pretty well established that No 117 was one of *two* locomotives at the head of the 100 ton train, the claim was still occasionally re-affirmed. But the circumstances of that unique effort have not been thoroughly authenticated. Evidence of the abilities of the 'Tennants' in 1888 indicates that only some very odd authority would have thought of using a two-cylinder compound in preference to a 'Tennant'. Or was it that someone said that he would feel happier if the engine of the racing train had a leading bogie? Was, in fact, a 'Tennant' attached to the train and the 4–4–0 placed in front of it as a literal 'pilot' that might be less likely than the 'Tennant' to leave the track at high speed?

The first ten Class F locomotives were built in 1887 and in the same year were also built ten engines of Class F1, generally similar to Class F but having single expansion in two inside cylinders. These classes had similar duties and their costs in coal and maintenance were no doubt carefully compared. If so, the outcome was a triumph for compounding inasmuch as T. W. Worsdell built fifteen more Class F compounds in 1890-1 but no more of Class F1. He then retired, and Wilson Worsdell eventually rebuilt all the Class F compounds as 'simples' with piston-valves and Stephenson valve-gear. So it seems either that compounding did not maintain any advantage in long service or that T. W. Worsdell had suffered some self-deception with a bias to compounding when comparing the performances of the first ten Fs and the first ten F1s.

Class G *(2-4-0)*
T. W. Worsdell built twenty 2-4-0s in 1887-8 and classified them as G. He had not decided at that time whether compounding was worth adopting and so he played safe by not adopting it in Class G. He was, however, pretty well 'sold' on Joy valve-gear, and so these engines were provided with it as the means of moving flat valves above the cylinders.

Class G had a drab and undistinguished career apart from being rebuilt as 4-4-0s with piston-valves and Stephenson gear by Wilson Worsdell from 1901, and apart from being known as 'Waterburys'. It must be added that in those days, the name 'Waterbury' was widely associated with a particular American make of watch. It is generally assumed now that the name was applied to Class G either because the engines were good time-keepers or (ironically) because they were not. Their running of trains by which E. L. Ahrons happened to travel left him with no high opinion of their capabilities, but why should it? They were not normally used for fast trains, but did their undistinguished work in pulling undistinguished trains at unexciting speeds. They were, in fact, just locomotive steam engines doing a useful job in transporting passengers who had no reason to take any special interest in their work.

They lasted for over twelve years in their original form, mostly pottering about in the York-Hull-Leeds triangle. Ahrons said he found them to be sluggish and that the enginemen did not like them. It could be expected that the rebuilding of Class G with piston-valves might diminish their sloth; some records of their running tend to bear this out, but they rarely reached the mile-a-minute rate on the level even with trivial trains.

Mr. C. J. Allen observed one unusual run by a Class G 4-4-0 and his account of it was published in the *Railway Magazine* for September 1914. The train was one booked to run non-stop from Bridlington to York and to cover the 47½ miles in an hour. Although composed of five vehicles it did not weigh more than 90 tons and so was not an overfacing burden for 'Waterbury' Class G No 521. Even so, she managed to spin out 16¾ minutes in climbing the 10 miles from Driffield to Enthorpe, and by Market Weighton had only 27 minutes left for the 22¼ level miles to York if she were to be in 'on time'.

But she went slower and slower, while turning out smoke and cinders, until she was down to 30 mph at Pocklington. Then someone on the footplate evidently moved the regulator to the 'Open' stop and in four miles No 521 was doing 69 mph. She blanched a little at this and dropped to 60, stimulating the driver to more severe action which spurred her to just over 71 mph. The 19¾ miles from Market Weighton to Earswick were covered in slightly more than 22 minutes in spite of crawling over the first few miles.

Mr. Allen, who had been surprised by such speed in a G, had no opportunity of asking the driver about this extraordinary performance and so could offer no explanation of it. The probability is that discord or incompetence on the footplate had persuaded or compelled an exasperated driver to ignore any union nonsense about demarcation and to do both footplate jobs himself. He ran slowly after Weighton while he shovelled a lot of coal into the firebox, then worked her up to seventy, eased her while he 'put a bit more on' and then opened out for a last fling. Skill and patience are kind to engines, but it's bad temper that really makes them go because for a time it obliterates consideration for their well-being.

Those whose knowledge of locomotive-work is limited to what they have read about it may be surprised at the suggestion that enginemen were not always perfectly placid gentlemen. Temper aroused by irritation was, however, as common on locomotives as anywhere else.

Another G, No 223, took four vehicles totalling 105 tons, from Hull to Bridlington, 30.9 miles in 37.8 minutes, slacking there to 20 mph and topping Flamborough bank at 27 mph. Down the other side 58 mph was touched and the train stopped at Filey, 44.2 miles in 59.2 minutes from Hull. This was a kind of 'residential express', so exclusive as not even to call at Bridlington.

Class H (*0-4-0T*)

Even after the North Eastern had been merged into the LNER, construction of locomotives of North Eastern design did not absolutely cease. In 1923 five engines of Class H were built to a design that originated in 1888 and had grown to a class of seventeen by 1897. These were small 0–4–0 tank engines, with inside cylinders, unusual with that arrangement because it means that the ash-pan must lie above cranks on the rear axle. In such a small engine this need not cause any trouble as the boiler could be set high enough to leave room for any reasonable depth of firebox and ashpan. In actual fact the boiler in Class H was kept down, and the firebox was shallow. The boiler was domeless only because it was to be interchangeable with that of the Class H1 0–6–0 tank engine with a crane.

These engines were made for use on sharply curved, lightly-laid lines as for example on docksides. They were also useful in roundhouse engine sheds, because each was short enough to stand on a turn-table with another engine of certain classes. Consequently a Class H could move a 'dead' engine from one radiating line to another; two 'live' engines would otherwise be required for this operation if there were only one entry-line to the turn-table.

An official 'diagram' for Class H specified the coal capacity as a meticulous 6¼ cwt, but as the engine had no bunker, it is more than usually difficult to justify such apparent precision. The official photograph shows No 982 with four lamps on brackets on the front but with no visible coal. It had to be carried on the side-tanks, and its conveyance to the fire would have been a serious problem if the engine had ever been required to make anything in the nature of a sustained effort.

Classes I and J (4–2–2)

Looking back at the 1880s, it is at first surprising to realize that T. W. Worsdell, after producing six new locomotive designs (three of them with simple/compound alternatives) should turn to 'single-wheelers'. The reason was that many fast, or moderately fast, passenger trains on routes without severe gradients, could be handled by tractive effort within the range of a 'single' with 17 or 18 tons on its driving wheels. So why use engines with driving wheels tied together by coupling rods where the simpler 'single' would do the job? The 'single' had certainly not been a favourite in earlier North Eastern days, but the higher axle-load permissible on the stronger track of later years altered the picture and a few 'singles' could find plenty of useful work.

Neither compounding nor Joy valve-gear seems (now) to be appropriate in a 'single' but T. W. Worsdell used both in Classes I and J. It was perhaps the bulky cylinder-block that persuaded him to use a leading bogie when many of the current 'singles' on other railways were 2–2–2s. He used inside bearings for the trailing axle as was natural enough, but in line with what was later found expedient with other classes of locomotive, outside bearings were substituted with other rebuilding later on. The last North Eastern locomotive design—the 'Pacific' of 1922—was destined to be altered in just the same way.

With cylinder-diameters totalling 42 inches in Class I, there was no room for valves between the cylinders, but they could be placed on top and in that position were conveniently worked by Joy valve-gear. Because the cylinders were of different diameters, and so wide overall that they would only just fit in between the frameplates, there was no lateral elbow-room and so the centre-lines of the cylinders were unsymmetrically placed in relation to the central vertical plane of the locomotive. This was Class I, about as simple as a compound locomotive could be, all neatly and smoothly finished in the Worsdell style, but perhaps a shade too tall in relation to its length to suggest a 'flyer'.

Not very long after the first Class I locomotive was built, someone thought that there was a place for something similar but a bit bigger, That 'bit' made it necessary to raise the rear of the grate to lie above the rear axle with a small 'pocket' in the ashpan and it also demanded an entirely different cylinder-block.

For in Class J the cylinder-diameters totalled 48 in and this was too much for the cylinders to lie side by side between the frameplates. The cylinders were therefore given different inclinations to the plane of the rail-heads; the centre-line of the large (LP) cylinder lay above the horizontal plane of the driving axle and the centre-line of the other cylinder lay below it. The cylinders could 'overlap' sufficiently not only to enable them to be got into the frame, but also to enable their centre-lines to be set at equal distances from the central vertical plane of the engine. This meant that the crank-axle could be used later with symmetrical placing of the cylinders when the engine was rebuilt as a plain two-cylinder simple.

A boiler mounted above a steam-chest on top of the large LP cylinder in its tipped-up position would have looked too high for stability and so the steam-chests were placed alongside the cylinders and outside the frame-plates, which had to be considerably cut away to admit them. This layout, adopted under duress, had the advantage that after removal of the steam-chest covers and the valves themselves, the port-faces were far more easily accessible for re-surfacing than they could ever be in any other arrangement of inside cylinders. And so also were the driving ends of the valve-spindles! They were ideally placed to be driven through link-motion by eccentrics carried on outward extensions of the driving axle, with all the valve-gear very readily accessible.

But it seemed that either the Worsdell ideal of external neatness or the Victorian obsession with hiding everything prohibited this mechanically ideal arrangement. For each cylinder, Joy valve-gear gave fore-and-aft reciprocation to a bulky 'crosshead' (see

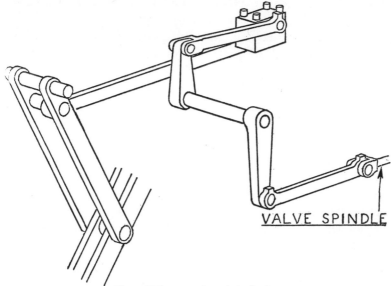

VALVE SPINDLE

Fig 2 Valve gear in original Class J

Fig 2) just behind the smokebox. A horizontal link, visible in many photographs, connected the crosshead to the top end of a rocking arm projecting upward from a rocking shaft that protruded through the frame-plate and carried at its outer end a longer arm projecting vertically downwards to move the valve through the medium of another horizontal link. A vertical plate prevented unauthorised persons from seeing this last stage of the mechanism.

In plan view, the radius-rod of the Joy valve-gear was offset from the centre of the curved guides and from the auxiliary cross-head. The first connecting link was offset from the crosshead on the other side of it. This layout was inexcusably bad when the alternative of direct link-motion was available and nobody could really have trusted it. Reported defects of the engines in service included broken valves (very unusual) and steam-chests cracked, probably by forces transmitted through them from the cylinder-block to the frame.

But before things got so far as that, and indeed before Class J went into regular service, two of them made test-runs with results that delighted North Eastern admirers and aroused rampant scepticism in others. (see Chapter 5).

Performance in service was not good enough for Wilson Worsdell and by 1894 Class J engines were being rebuilt as two-cylinder simples, with 8 in outside-admission piston-valves as close together as possible above the cylinders. The valves were inclined downwards to the rear at 1 in 6.5 while the cylinders sloped upwards at 1 in 22. The valves were worked by link motion directly except for a lateral offset of $3\frac{1}{2}$ in. As the centre-lines of 8 in piston-valves cannot be set much nearer together than about 12 in, and as the cranks prevented two sets of link motion from being set so far apart as this, lateral offset in the connection between link-block and valve was unavoidable.

But, details apart, the rebuilt Class J was so very much superior in general arrangement to the two-cylinder compounds and to Class M1 with its outside steam-chests that it impressed North Eastern men in much the same way as Whale's 'Precursors' gladdened North Western men.

In their simplified form these 4-2-2s could run fast, but their normal duties on secondary passenger trains did not demand high speed and in those days train-timing enthusiasts were not so numerous that any occasional bit of sparkle had much chance of being recorded. Nevertheless in the *Railway Magazine* from December 1913, Mr. C. J. Allen reported No 1523 to have run from Leeds to Scarborough in a net time of $69\frac{1}{2}$ minutes for $67\frac{1}{2}$ miles. On the way, speed was worked up to 85 mph in a few miles down 1 in 150 between Micklefield and Church Fenton. After having been braked to get round the curve at that station, the engine attained 74 mph on the level between there and York. But this was with a load of only about 80 tons, markedly different from the 224 tons behind No 1518 on the test-run in 1890, and so it was in no sense any approach to a confirmation of the high speeds reported in connection with that run.

Class K (0-6-0T)
Specially built for use on the Hull dock-lines was Class K, a smaller version of Class H. At first a cylindrical boiler with

internal fire-grate was used. (This might be very loosely termed a 'marine' boiler.) Later on this was replaced by a boiler somewhat similar to that of Class H.

Class M1 (4-4-0)

Wilson Worsdell must have seen enough of his brother's compound engines to realise that compounding was best left alone and he was not captivated by Joy valve-gear. He could hardly fail to appreciate one great advantage of outside steam chests (or 'valve chests') as used on the Class J compound 'singles'. This was the easy accessibility of the valves. You stood on the ground near the bogie and found, at about head height, the valve-chest cover with about twenty studs looking at you. Removal of those studs allowed the cover to be taken off, and there was the back of the valve right in front of your eyes. The contrast between this and the impossibility of obtaining any comparable view of the valves in any conventional placing of the valve-chests was probably what decided Wilson Worsdell to use outside valve-chests on his next design of locomotive. This was the M1 class 4-4-0 which, with extended smokebox and the usual Worsdell cab, was probably the most impressive-looking British locomotive of its day.

Each valve was moved by Stephenson link motion between the frame-plates through drop-arms and a rocking shaft that reached out through a hole in the frame-plate. The alternative of direct drive from Stephenson gear outside the frame was not impossible although not so easy as it would have been in a 'single-driver' with no coupling-rod in the way. But outside valve-gear was very rare in Britain and indeed in America at that time and Worsdell was probably restrained by respect for convention from thus making the valve-gear as easily accessible as the valve itself. There was, however, adequate precedent for such an arrangement in locomotives on the continent of Europe.

The last M1, No 1639, differed from the others in having piston-valves of a particular design evolved by W. M. Smith of the North Eastern staff, in collaboration with corresponding men on the staff of the Midland Railway. Each 'segmental' valve-head was ingeniously made in a number of bits and pieces, designed to collapse under such high cylinder-pressure as might be developed by trapped water before it became high enough to burst the cylinder-covers. This was just one of a score of 'gadgets' developed (some were patented) over the ensuing thirty years or more by many inventors with the same objects in view. Only with extreme and prolonged reluctance did locomotive engineers in general admit that the best solution to this problem was to use simple solid valve-heads and to allot the job of prohibiting dangerously high pressure to a relief valve on the cylinder-cover itself.

No 1639 was reported to have burned $29\frac{1}{2}$ lb of coal per mile as against an average of 34 lb per mile by eight Class M1 engines with flat valves. It would have been more convincing if five engines with piston-valves had averaged 13 per cent lower coal-consumption than five with flat valves. A single engine, handled by a conscientious crew and known to be under special observation may readily get along on 10 to 15 per cent less coal than the average of a group of nominally identical engines not specially watched.

The most dramatic performance by an M1 was that extracted from No 1620 by driver R. Nicholson in taking 105 tons from Newcastle to Edinburgh in 113* minutes at a start-to-stop average of 66 mph in the early morning of 22 August 1895.

But immediately before this, the same train had been brought from York to Newcastle in $78\frac{1}{2}$ minutes at a start-to-stop average of $61\frac{1}{2}$ mph by M1 No 1621 in charge of driver G. Turner. The most unnerving part of this trip was the average of 74 mph over the last 8.66 miles from Chester-le-Street including three sharp curves within sight of Newcastle Central. Relevant to this was an observation by Mr. H. A. Watson (who later became General Superintendent of the North Eastern Railway) that the train ran so slowly alongside the platform at Newcastle that No 1620, which followed it in as soon as reversal of the points allowed, touched the buffers of the last vehicle before it stopped. With

*Some say 114, some say 115; no one really knows.

64

such a slow stop, the last mile of running round the three curves can hardly have taken less than $1\frac{1}{2}$ minutes in which case the average over the preceding 7.66 miles was 83.6 mph. Mr. Watson noted that the train was at rest in Newcastle Central for only $1\frac{1}{2}$ minutes.

Onward to Edinburgh, intermediate times recorded to the nearest minute in the guard's journal show nothing inconsistent with the overall average but an implied average of 83.6 mph from Belford to Berwick looks rather high and, rather oddly, is identical with the estimated speed of No 1621 in coming down to Gateshead. This, however, is technically unimportant as the real measure of the performance is the time taken to complete the journey, and this would naturally be checked by times taken by station officials from the station-clocks.

The one important question that may be asked about a long trip made at a much higher speed average than usual concerns the running in places where there were formal speed restrictions imposed by consideration of safety on curves. Between Newcastle and Edinburgh there were such restrictions at Morpeth and at Berwick. The latter was a very severe one in 1895 (it was later eased by re-location of tracks) and it might be of some interest to know how fast Nicholson ran through these restricted regions during the 113-minute run at the record-breaking average, for this course, of 66 mph. There is absolutely no factual information on this point but it is unlikely that the train was brought down to the official limits as these, like all others on British railways, were deliberately set on the low ('safe') side. What happens in practice is that through long'years of running, engine drivers decide for themselves from the reactions of engines what are the highest comfortable speeds for various classes. They could not specify those speeds in miles per hour and would not in any case admit to anything over the official maximum, but however reckless Nicholson may be suspected to have been, his judgment was justified to the extent that no harm befell anyone. Moreover, the possible saving in time by over-fast running through Morpeth and through Berwick is negligible compared with the total of 113 minutes, and so it need raise no question about the merit of the performance of the locomotive. No steam engine is known to have made the journey in shorter time.

A 'star' performance by a locomotive on a special occasion tends to cast a cloud over its subsequent work and that of her sisters in ordinary service. When in later years anyone observed an M1 to lose time on some trifling job, he was bound to ask himself what could have brought the engine to such a 'low' condition. Or what sort of restrictive practices the enginemen were adopting to make her so slow?

Certainly the average work of Class M1 wins it no distinguished place in locomotive history. They were good solid, stolid British 4-4-0s driven by men who would deny any possibility of running from Newcastle to Edinburgh in 113 minutes or even 130 minutes. The record time was achieved by men who rather liked 'hard running' (enginemen never used the word 'fast' in any such connection as this), were used to it and were delighted to have a chance to do it on an occasion when officials might be more inclined to applaud than to criticize.

Class M   (C/4-4-0)
converted to Class 3CC (3C/4-4-0)

Perhaps to show some respect for his brother's devotion to compounding, Wilson Worsdell built a two-cylinder compound equivalent of Class M1. Its running number, 1619, suggested that its design may have preceded that of Class M1, but it was not completed until at least three M1s were running.

The cylinder-arrangement of No 1619 was substantially that of the Class J 'singles' but the valves were worked by Stephenson gear and rocking shafts as in Class M1.

Coal-consumption of No 1619 was reported to be about $30\frac{1}{2}$ lb per mile as against an average of 34 lb per mile by standard flat-valve M1s on similar work. Differences of this order had failed to restrain Wilson Worsdell from converting two-cylinder compounds to two-cylinder 'simples' and so it was no surprise to learn that No 1619 had been withdrawn from service in 1898 for 'conversion.'

The conversion was, however, to a three-cylinder compound

in a form that came to be associated with the name 'Smith', an appropriately ordinary name for a scheme that was obviously the best of possible alternative arrangements of three cylinders in a compound 4–4–0 locomotive.

In the rebuilt No 1619, the high-pressure cylinder on the centre-line of the engine was fed by a piston-valve below it, but there was no room to provide piston-valves for the (outside) low-pressure cylinders except above them. Joy valve-gear or Walschaerts valve-gear might have worked them in that position, but the former had passed out of North Eastern favour and the latter was never to gain it convincingly. So flat valves were provided for the low-pressure cylinders.

But the 'conversion' of No 1619 did not stop at the cylinders. A new boiler was provided with grate area of 23.7 sq ft, which was an advance of 20 per cent on that of the original boiler. This could give the engine a very substantial advantage over Class M1 with one proviso.

The longer grate was too long to lie in front of the rear axle and so its rear end had to lie above the rear axle. As the centre-height of the boiler-barrel was not appreciably increased, this higher position of the grate meant that the firebox was shallow and its heating surface was rather less than that of the Class M1 firebox, and the lower edge of the fire-hole was only 17 in above the firebars. Moreover, the centre of the rear end of the brick arch was only about 27 in above the firebars. The firebox was similar to that of Class S; see Fig. 4, page 70.

To get the best out of a fire in a box of this kind called for more careful firing than was necessary or useful in firing the deep boxes on other North Eastern engines. Given such care, No 1619 might well produce considerably more power than could be expected of Class M1. But if the fireman resented the unaccustomed restrictions of the new firebox and made no effort to accommodate his methods to them, No 1619 might well fall below Class M1 standards of performance.

At one stage, the rebuilt No 1619 had 'cross water-tubes' in the upper part of the firebox. These were $1\frac{3}{4}$ inches in diameter, arranged in three groups of seven, extending across the upper

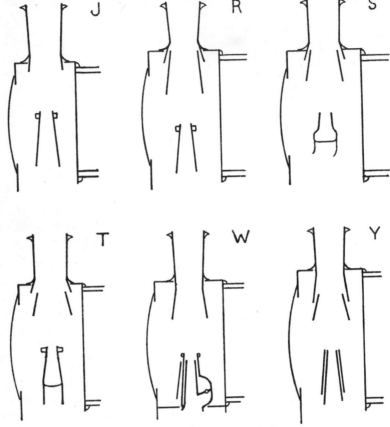

Fig 3 Some North Eastern smokeboxes

part of the firebox. To give access to them for washing-out, the outer firebox had three manholes and covers on each side. These projected outside the line of the lagging plates and were covered by flattish domes mildly suggestive of ulcerations. This experiment did not persist; evidently it was found at Gateshead, as elsewhere, that cross water-tubes were not worth the trouble they caused.

It is interesting to note that the original driving wheels were retained and determined the stroke of 24 in for the outside pistons. There was no corresponding restriction on the stroke of the inside piston as a new crank-axle was necessary in any case; a 26 in stroke was adopted.

The best comment that can be made about the performance of No 1619 in her three-cylinder form is that the North Eastern built no other engine like her. In attempting to assess the significance of this, one must remember that Wilson Worsdell found reason to convert many two-cylinder compound engines to single-expansion and may have had an anti-compounding bias. One must also remember that a third cylinder on a locomotive, like a third man on the footplate, must confer some substantial advantage if it is to justify the nuisance it causes. Over forty years later Darlington and Doncaster were being reminded of an old dictum that there is no point in placing three cylinders in an engine if you can get by with two.

The rebuilt No 1619 introduced a change in 'styling' of the driving-wheel splashers. One huge splasher built out to the cab side-sheets enclosed the top halves of two driving wheels and the intervening space as usual in Worsdell practice, but brass strip ran in two separate semicircles matching the wheels. Small splashers, well cut out, were provided for the ends of the coupling-rods. At this distance in time, it is hard to understand how compliance with convention should be so strong as to prohibit the raising of the running board to avoid any need for this complication and to make the top slide-bars permanently visible.

Furthermore, the boiler lagging-plates matched the smokebox, whereas in existing North Eastern practice, there was a marked difference in diameter and a brass ring in this region.

Classes 66 190 957 (2-2-4T)

The 2-2-4T is a rarely used wheel arrangement but it happened that it survived on the North Eastern in the form of 'Officer's Special Tank Engines'.

Of these No 66 *Aerolite* is by far the best known because it has been on exhibition in York Museum since 1934. It is also perhaps the prettiest of the lot. It is moreover the only one of them to be a two-cylinder compound. It has an extraordinary history of repeated and extensive rebuilding.

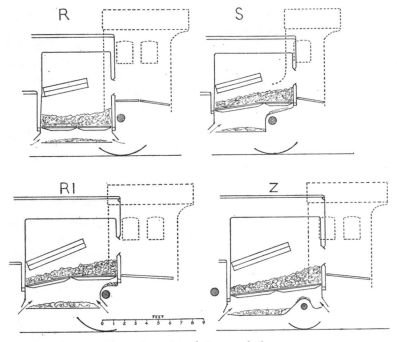

Fig 4 Some North Eastern fireboxes

It started as a ramshackle, outside-frame 2–2–2T produced by
Fletcher in 1869. In 1886 it was nominally rebuilt by T. W.
Worsdell as a trim little outside frame 2–2–2T. Whether this
contained any part of the Fletcher engine but the wheels is very
doubtful. It was rebuilt as a two-cylinder compound and, probably because the leading wheels left insufficient space for the
larger cylinder block, the wheel arrangement was altered to
4–2–2T. This is said to have been done in 1892, but this is hard
to believe as Wilson Worsdell had by that time been in charge
of North Eastern steam for some two years and had been 'anti-
compound' for much longer. Some date before the retirement of
T. W. Worsdell in 1890 would be more readily credible.

The last rebuilding was by Wilson Worsdell in 1902. This
included the provision of an entirely new frame and reversal of
the wheel arrangement to 2–2–4T which left room for a much
larger bunker than before.

Among the many interesting features of this beautifully finished engine is the enclosure of the Westinghouse air-pump in a varnished wooden cupboard in the cab.

The top of the boiler is not so high as the tops of the tanks and some observers may regard this as a visual blemish. The fact that the engine is a two-cylinder compound is not immediately obvious but there is no difficulty in the Museum in confirming this by examining the cylinder-ends. One notices that the larger piston has a tail-rod whilst the other has not. From the cab one may notice that the tops of the side-tanks are tied together by a plate that spans the boiler behind the dome. One may also form the impression that this little engine would have been a gorgeous vehicle for exploring the old North Eastern Railway. It had the easy job of pulling the engineer's inspection coach. The writer once saw the combination running on one of the subsidiary lines parallel to the main-line north of Severus Junction at York and was impressed by its very free motion without steam on the level. The young railway enthusiast might think it the height of luxurious pleasure to be whirled about the system in such a sumptuous equipage. One may surmise, however, that the official to whom it 'belonged' used it only when urgent business made it necessary and that he generally preferred to stay in his office.

The other long surviving 2–4–4Ts of Classes 190 and 957 were rather larger engines than *Aerolite*. Of the former class, No 1679 was withdrawn in 1931 but No 190 lasted till the end of 1936.

The Class 957 engine (No 957) was in its later years stationed at Hull. It occasionally ran two-coach passenger trains (to York, for example) in temporary replacement of self-propelled rail coaches, and so remained as the last British 'single' in service till it was scrapped in 1937.

Class O *(0–4–4T)*
Although it might be thought that for service with as much backward running as forward running a four-coupled eight-wheel tank engine should be a 2–4–2T, many locomotive engineers favoured the 0–4–4T and the Class O originated by

Worsdell in 1894 was one of the most highly esteemed tank engine types ever to run in Great Britain. They inspired something like affection in enginemen and may be compared in this way with the M7 class 0-4-4Ts of the London & South Western Railway.

Points in favour of the 0-4-4T were firstly that as the firebox lay between the bogie and the nearer coupled axle, it could be deep and could have a deep ash-pan, secondly that no ordinary unevenness in the track could make any perceptible difference to the weight on the coupled wheels and thirdly that reduction in the weight of water in the tanks made little difference to front-axle loading and not much difference to the load on the crank-axle. The adhesion weight of a 0-4-4T therefore suffered less reduction by unfavourable circumstances than did that of a 2-4-2T.

The inspiration for Class O may well have come from the Fletcher Class BTP of which over a hundred were in North Eastern service when Wilson Worsdell took over but there were also sixty of T. W. Worsdell's Class A 2-4-2Ts running by the end of 1892.

Much of Wilson Worsdell's locomotive development was rather pointedly opposed to that of his brother. This may have represented sheer difference in technical opinion, or it may have been a means of letting everyone know that 'TW' was not the only Worsdell who could think for himself. Whatever the reason, Wilson Worsdell built 110 0-4-4Ts of the same general dimensions as the existing 2-4-2Ts and there was nothing in the performance of the two classes to suggest that this was unwise.

Class O worked well with passenger trains whether doing a mile a minute on the flat or struggling up 1 in 40 at a quarter of a mile a minute. A good deal of the latter was done between Scarborough and Whitby. It seemed so arduous that Wilson Worsdell and Vincent Raven between them evolved a 4-6-2T for that route, but much of the work there continued to be done by Class O engines because the newer giants were not always convincingly superior.

At one time or another Class O tank engines worked short-distance passenger trains wherever such trains ran on the North Eastern Railway. They took expresses between Newcastle and Middlesbrough, suburban trains out of Newcastle, Leeds and Hull and country branch trains to places like Pateley Bridge and Hawes Junction. As LNER Class G5 they continued their good work after grouping and only seven out of 110 had been withdrawn by the end of 1947.

Class Q (4-4-0)

It is difficult to draw any significant distinction between Class Q and Class M1 as the dimensions were virtually identical. That the LNER had similar difficulty when classifying its locomotives soon after its formation in 1923 is suggested by its registering the two classes as D17/2 and D17/1.

As the North Eastern was beginning to regard piston valves as desirable at the time when Class Q was being designed, it seems odd that the engines were given flat valves over the cylinders, with Stephenson gear and rocking shafts to work the valves. This scheme was a cross between T. W. Worsdell's Joy gear with flat valves and Wilson Worsdell's Stephenson gear directly driving piston-valves.

A feature very noticeable by the eye was the application of clerestory roofs to the cabs. It was almost an admission, and a pretty florid one, that North Eastern cabs were sometimes a little hot for the men. It was, however, an expensive way of providing ventilation openings and it was never applied to any North Eastern engine outside Classes Q and Q1. A small trap door in the roof, just behind the whistles, provided all the adjustable top ventilation in most North Eastern cabs.

With Class Q was introduced on the North Eastern the practice of fitting brass rims to the chimneys of the more 'important' classes. This was continued until the completion of the first twenty of Class Z in 1911.

Class Q1 (4-4-0)

In contrast to Class Q, for which there was no obvious justification, Class Q1 comprised two locomotives built for a specific

73

purpose. This was to provide 'flyers' for use in any 'Race to Scotland' that might develop in 1896 or afterwards. It is true that the race in 1895 had ended in what amounted to a truce between East and West, but the East had been—just—defeated and with a little more speed and determination might not have been. So there was reason for building locomotives capable of use in general service, but also more suitable for really fast running than were the fastest standard North Eastern four-coupled engines.

In the nineteenth century, the homely recipe for higher speed was bigger wheels and so an easy design-procedure for the North Eastern was to build a Q with two pairs of driving wheels like those of the Class J 'singles'. These wheels, 7 feet 7 inches in diameter, were the largest coupled wheels ever to be used in Britain. (We were beaten in this line by France where there was once a 0–6–0 with 8 ft 2 in wheels).

No railway racing in quite so blatant a form as that of 1895 ever occurred afterwards, and Class Q1 was never specifically tested for the attribute particularly desired in it, but most students of the locomotive admire its well set up aggressive lines.

The two engines of Class Q1 performed similar duties to those allotted to Class Q over thirty-four years and so may be regarded as having justified themselves, even though they never had any chance of defending the reputation of their builders and owners by racing.

Class R   (4–4–0)

Wilson Worsdell had built about fifty 4–4–0s between 1887 and 1897. Among them, Class M1 had the distinction, when first built, of being the heaviest passenger train tender engine in Britain, and during the 1895 'Race to Scotland' one of them had run at a sustained rate that only a North Western 'Precedent' had beaten. Classes Q and Q1 had clerestory cab-roofs and Class Q1 had exceptionally big wheels. They were all good-looking engines but it cannot be traced that their speed or power in ordinary service was anything more than adequate.

In 1899 the slightly larger Class R was introduced; in eight

74

years it had been built up to a total of sixty and at that time there were fewer than twenty larger main line passenger train locomotives on the North Eastern. These figures, and others relating to the performance of various members of Class R, suggest that the engines were very distinctly superior to the other North Eastern 4–4–0s.

The main difference, apart from a small one in size, between Class R and its predecessors was the use of piston-valves instead of flat valves. The circumference of an $8\frac{3}{4}$ in piston-valve is so much greater than the port-width of about 17 in for a 19 in cylinder that, for a given valve-lap and given cut-off, the area of the port-opening in Class R might well be 25 per cent greater than that in any other North Eastern 4–4–0. So the dimensions of the piston-valve could permit the use of an earlier cut-off, and therefore more economical use of steam, for any particular job, than was possible in an engine with flat valves.

In Class R the piston-valves were set as close together as possible below the cylinders and were worked by the usual link motion directly except for a lateral offset of $3\frac{1}{2}$ inches. The valve-spindles were only slightly inclined to the plane of the rails, but the cylinders were set at 1 in 11 downwards to the rear. The valves were 'segmental' which means that each valve-head had packing rings each made in several pieces arranged so as to yield under excessive cylinder-pressure that might otherwise burst the cylinder-covers, which were, however, fitted with 2 in. relief-valves to make sure.

It is strange that the valves were arranged to give 'outside admission' as this subjects the valve-spindle glands to full steam pressure with the consequent possibility of much more serious leakage of steam than would have been the case with the usual 'inside admission'. Coal-consumption of 45 lb per mile by Class R engines in their early days was not specially creditable.

Piston tail-rods, not encased in tubes, were provided in Class R. To give clearance for the tail-rods, the curved slope of the running board under the smokebox was cut away in the middle, and a box-like projection covered the gap.

The firebox, entirely ahead of the rear axle, was 39 in deep from the lower edge of the firehole to the firebars; the ash-pan had plenty of volume and a damper back and front. The lower edge of the brick arch at its rear end was at the same height as the top of the fire-hole. So the engine was easy to fire, either with a fire-bed of uniform depth (right for maximum power) or with a tapered fire (for ease and comfort regardless of speed) that needed feeding only at the back.

The blast nozzle was below the centre-line of the boiler. It discharged steam into a convergent petticoat pipe just below the divergent cone of the chimney.

Figures published in the *Railway Magazine* show that Class R engines could pull and run very satisfactorily. They did not quite equal North Western 4–4–0s in pulling nor Great Western 4–4–0s in high speed but they met North Eastern needs for some years. As an example—perhaps an exceptional one—of the work of a Class R engine (No 2011, the first to be built) with a 15-coach train of about 340 tons, mention may be made of a report by Mr. Charles Rous-Marten of a run from Newcastle to Darlington, 36.5 miles in 44.7 minutes, start to stop, followed immediately by a journey on to York, 44.1 miles in 48.5 minutes. This was in the year 1900.

The last R to be built, No 1672, for many years held the speed-record for the Darlington–York stretch, having covered it start-to-stop in 39 minutes 34 seconds with a load of 165 tons. A feature of this run was a very fast start, the first 5.2 miles to Eryholme being covered in 6 minutes 14 seconds, a full minute less than the usual time for the train concerned, which was the 'fastest train in the British Empire' in 1913. No 1672 was at the time a 'wet steam' engine.

Class R No 1207, fitted with a superheater, took a 135 ton train over the course in a net time of 40 minutes and ran for four miles on the level at 80 mph in a strong south-west wind.

These runs were reported in the *Railway Magazine* for July 1913 by Mr. C. J. Allen. In January 1915 he gave details of what must have been a rather exciting run by Class R No 476 with a 315 ton train from Harrogate to Darlington. The route encourages fast running as the first two miles are downhill at 1 in 66 and further on are four miles down at 1 in 133. The train passed Ripon (11½ miles) in 11½ minutes having touched 82 mph on the 1 in 133. There was necessarily a severe reduction of speed in getting onto the main line at Northallerton where the train was nevertheless half a minute inside 'even time' from the start. The first stop was just short of Darlington in rather less than 41 minutes for 39¼ miles from Harrogate.

These figures show that Class R could be lively engines and their number proves that they gave satisfaction on a good many North Eastern passenger train services.

The second item in Table 1 shows one of them, even though using 'wet' steam at the time, to have produced as much power in relation to its size as many of the best superheated engines in other British railways.

A report that the first Class R engine No 2011 ran 284,000 miles before returning to the works for general repairs has little significance for anyone who does not know what was usual in this respect. When it is mentioned that anything over 60,000 miles was regarded as highly satisfactory, the reaction to this reported performance by No 2011 is that of admiration followed by wonder and perhaps by incredulity.

After the year 1948, British Railways were attaching much importance to high mileage between successive major repairs and hoped by taking special care in design, in choice of materials and in techniques in minor repairs to make 100,000 miles the normally achieved distance between visits of locomotives to the works for repairs. Several locomotives reached this figure occasionally, but the average in 1953 for some 30 classes of British locomotives was less than 90,000 miles, and the maximum was 97,000 miles for LMS Class 5 4-6-0s, except for the 104,000 miles achieved by BR Class 2 2-6-0s on very light work.

North Eastern No 2011, according to a note in the *Locomotive Magazine* for November 15, 1920 beat the general average figure in a ratio well over 3 and the best figure in the ratio 2.75. The engine ran 455 miles per day, five days per week and 161 miles on one day a week; the seventh day was occupied in 'washing-out'. This left little time for much more than light repairs and one may reasonably assume that the routine was broken whenever any more extensive maintenance action became necessary.

The engine was in Gateshead shed every night, not far from Gateshead works and one wonders whether this proximity was a help in creating this remarkable mileage record. Another feature was that the working of No 2011 was entrusted to two pairs of men and confined to them. When each man knew that he was going to have this same engine for an average of three days a week for years, he recognized that it was worth while to him to do everything in the best possible way and not to tolerate misuse or waste of any kind. And perhaps the trips made by No 2011, although long, were with light loads.

These circumstances, plus a bit of luck, could explain how No 2011 might be able to run a much-greater-than-average mileage between successive major repairs. But 284,000? No other Class R engine was claimed to have come within 130,000 miles of it! Can anyone be chided for placing a large question mark behind 284,000?

Class R1 (4-4-0)

It is not hard to see what persuaded Wilson Worsdell to build some big 4-4-0s in 1908 nor, looking at the sectional drawing published in *The Locomotive* for April 11, 1909 is it hard to see why Class R1 as originally built was going to leave something to be desired.

The Class R 4-4-0s had been so satisfactory that by the end of 1907 sixty of them had been built. The only bigger passenger train engines the North Eastern had at that time were the 'Atlantics' which, with a grate area of some 27 sq ft had basically some 30 per cent more power than Class R but they did not show this very convincingly in service. With a trailing axle that could make the adhesion weight uncertain when trying to pull hard on the imperfect track in the vicinity of large stations, they were probably inferior to Class R engines in 'getting away' with heavy trains. So why not shorten the barrel of the Class V boiler and mount it on a 4-4-0 chassis? And why not place the valves between the cylinders and the smokebox instead of on the wrong side of the cylinders as they were in Class R? And what about working steam at 225 lb per sq in as Churchward was doing at Swindon?

When it had been decided to adopt these suggestions, it was a fairly simple job for the drawing office to start from the chassis of Class R, to turn the cylinder-block upside down with valves enlarged to 10 in diameter, and to mount on top a shortened version of the Class V boiler as low down as possible without cramping anything too much. This made a large and imposing 4-4-0 with 42 tons on the coupled wheels. What was specially notable about this was axle-loading exceeding 20 tons for the first time in a British locomotive; the figure of 21 tons was never exceeded in any other two-cylinder engine in this country.

The T. W. Worsdell type of comprehensive splasher for the driving wheels was abandoned and on each side separate splashers were united by an inverted trough set high enough to clear the coupling rod. The Westinghouse pump was mounted on the running-board alongside the smoke-box on the driver's side of the engine.

The smokebox was mounted on a saddle but instead of extending it forward so that it could contain spark-arresting plates on the American Master Mechanics' plan, ten inclined slats were mounted in front of the tubeplate and ten more on the smokebox door in the hope of persuading sparks to go down instead of up.

The nozzle of the blast-pipe was $4\frac{3}{4}$ inches in diameter inside and was surrounded by a $7\frac{1}{2}$ in diameter annulus into the bottom of which part of the exhaust steam coming from the cylinders could be diverted by a butterfly valve under the control of the driver. So the effective diameter of the nozzle might be anything between $4\frac{3}{4}$ in and $7\frac{1}{2}$ in, the corresponding cross-sectional areas having a ratio of $2\frac{1}{2}$. But such draught was normally needed that nothing but the smallest orifice sufficed and this elaborate blast-pipe (with the char-lifting auxiliary mentioned on p 110) was soon replaced by an ordinary one.

The firebox, 9 ft long outside, was too long to be placed between the coupled axles but the ashpan was shortened so as to fit in, with the result that 20 in of the length of the grate was behind the rear air inlet to the ashpan and the underside of the firebars was only 6 in above this part of the ashpan. (See Fig 4 p. 70). After this space became filled with ash, the effective grate-area was about 18 per cent less than the quoted figure. The front half of the grate sloped downwards by about 8 in. The fire-hole was set with its lower edge about two feet above the back ends of the firebars. Any ordinary fireman who thus had the task of lifting shovelfuls of coal to that height was not going to throw it hard as well unless compelled, and so he would naturally build a firebed sloping down from fire-hole height at the back to about 6 in above the firebars at the front. He could then lob shovelfuls of coal through the firehole and the bigger pieces would tend to roll down to the front while the vibration of the engine tended to shuffle the whole fire-bed in the same direction. Distribution of the coal in the firebox tended to be automatic and the fireman did not need to think about it. But while the rear part of the fire-bed was acting partly as a hopper and partly as the top section of a straight helter-skelter, it was not generating much heat. The greater part of the combustion took place on the sloping part of the grate. The effective grate area was therefore about 16 sq ft or 20 per cent less than that of a Class R carefully fired. So long as the power required was no more than proportionate to this, conditions on a Class R1 were reasonable. But when the engine was required to produce power commensurate with its size, the combustion-rate in the front part of the fire was very high so that loss of fuel in cinders carried into the smokebox became very serious. Class R1 locomotives were known as 'Miners' friends' at a time when the need of miners was for work.

It is hard to understand how matters of this kind were apparently ignored by locomotive-designers but the fact is that some of them had never ridden on a locomotive, much less attempted to fire one. Most of the British chief mechanical engineers had had such experience, but so far back in time and therefore on such small locomotives that the labour and difficulties of firing a big engine may never have been considered by them.

Designers might have enlightened themselves on the subject of throttling of engine fires by ash if they added to their drawings, sketches of the fire-bed and of the probable accumulation of ash in the ashpan. In this connection it is useful to realize that the coefficient of friction of cinders on steel roughened by corrosion is very high indeed, so that a slope that is to be self-clearing has to be very much steeper than one might at first suppose. Inadequate pessimism on this point caused the very last British Railways standard design, completed in 1954, to suffer trouble by ashpan choking of the type that had throttled innumerable earlier locomotives of which Class R1 was an example.

The Class R1 4-4-0s were large, neat, handsome locomotives that could be 'bashed' along to some purpose by willing and able crews but they were heavy on coal and so were not liked by anyone. Ten of them were built as an initial batch and nobody wanted any more.

High boiler-pressure means high maintenance-cost for the boiler and the 225 psi in Class R1 was soon abandoned in favour of 200 psi. When superheaters were applied to the engines, the diameter of the cylinders was increased and the boiler-pressure reduced to 180 psi.

A couple of runs with superheated Class R1 engines showed them able to maintain 64 mph on the level with a load of about 360 tons. This satisfied most North Eastern requirements but it was not brilliant by comparison with the work of superheater-fitted locomotives of comparable size on other British railways.

In their early days, the R1s were used on the 'best' North Eastern passenger trains, but increases in the number of 'Atlantics' displaced them to secondary service. In view of the achievements of British 4-4-0s many years later, it is sad to realize that only imperfections in what must have looked like details prevented Class R1 from being multiplied to do all the work for which 'Atlantics' were built later on.

Class 4CC (4C/4-4-2)
The North Eastern's two four-cylinder compound 'Atlantics' were undoubtedly inspired by W. M. Smith and their Belpaire

fireboxes (the only ones on North Eastern engines) probably represented a bit of borrowing from Johnson on the Midland, as was the arrangement of three safety-valves.

In these engines the four cylinders were in line abreast under the smokebox and each was fed by a piston valve above it. Two sets of valve-gear sufficed as the two valves in each half of the width had a common reciprocating motion. The outer valves for the high-pressure cylinders had 'inside admission' and the others, for the low pressure cylinders, had 'outside admission'. This difference was necessary because of the opposed motions of the corresponding pistons. It was also useful in that it subjected no valve-spindle gland to boiler-pressure and that it resulted in the simplest possible paths for steam through the cylinder-block.

The diameter of the boiler-barrel was 6 in less than that of the Class V 'Atlantics' but the outside length and outside width of the firebox were the same in both classes. The official figure of 29 sq ft quoted for the grate area of Class CC4 implied that the width of water-space had been reduced from 3 in to 2 in in the 4CC. This was not a move in the right direction.

The valves of No 730 were worked by conventional link motion, while No 731 had Walschaerts valve-gear. The latter engine does not figure in any official records of test-runs or in any published record of running in ordinary service. In the *Railway Magazine* for December 1907 Mr. Charles Rous-Marten gave details of two undistinguished runs by No 730 and mentioned that one by No 731 called for no special comment. In the *Locomotive Magazine* for November 1907 it is recorded that No 731 took a Royal train from York to Edinburgh with a four-minute stop at Newcastle. This was believed to be the first time any engine had worked a train over the $204\frac{1}{2}$ miles in this direction although No 730 is said to have made the corresponding journey in the opposite direction with another Royal train a year earlier.

In a dynamometer-car test No 730, hauling 475 tons, passed Darlington in 49 minutes from a start at York and this was high-class work by comparison with contemporary British running in ordinary service; the highest speeds attained on the way were 61 mph at Danby Wiske and 64 mph on the down grade past Croft

Spa. When running steadily at about 56 mph near Tollerton, the recorded cut-off figures were 41 per cent in the HP cylinders and 54 per cent in the LP cylinders; this corresponds to an overall expansion ratio equivalent to a cut-off of 20 to 25 per cent in a non-compound engine and this is about the most economical operating range.

The test was one of a series made with the object of establishing the relative haulage capacities of Classes R, S1, V and 4CC. That of 4CC in relation to R was exactly the same as the ratio of the officially-quoted grate areas, suggesting that in this respect compounding gave no advantage.

Class V was not so good as Classes R and 4CC in relation to grate area, while Class S1 was hardly superior to Class R even without taking account of grate area.

In other dynamometer-car tests, southbound from Darlington, No 730 took 455 tons, a Class V engine took 398 tons and a Class R engine 365 tons. Over the 37.3 miles from Eryholme to Poppleton Junction the average speeds were 63.7, 67.3 and 61.3 mph. On the basis of drawbar horsepower per square foot of grate area the relative figures are 31, 32 and 33. So the Class R beat the others in this respect, but the range of uncertainty in estimated power prohibits any insistence that this was the real order of excellence. There was very little in it.

Although No 730 did well in these tests, the results could hardly be held to justify building any more Class 4CC engines in view of their high cost in construction and maintenance. A marked saving in coal might have justified it, but there is no evidence that any such thing was ever demonstrated on the North Eastern.

When built, and for a few years afterwards, No 730 may well have been the best main line passenger locomotive on the North Eastern, but when Class Z 'Atlantics' became established, that was certainly not the case and the compounds ceased to be used on the top-rank passenger trains.

It is perhaps worth mentioning that the front tube-plate in Class 4CC was some 30 in to the rear of the usual position at the front end of the boiler lagging-plates. Thus the boiler was shorter than it looked, and the smokebox longer than it looked.

Class S (2/4-6-0)

The 'four-coupled bogie express passenger locomotive' was well established in Great Britain before the end of the nineteenth century and it was inevitable that soon somebody was going to produce a 'six-coupled bogie' locomotive for passenger service. As this had already been done in America, Wilson Worsdell with his American associations was perhaps the likeliest man to do it. Jones, on the Highland, had already adopted the 2/4-6-0 for goods service and it was only one very shallow step thence to the same sort of engine for faster running.

So it was no real surprise that in 1899 Gateshead Works turned out No 2001, the first of the Class S that, with some modifications, eventually totalled forty engines. A driving wheel diameter of 6 ft 1 in was not in the 'express' class by the standards of those days, and indeed few of these locomotives ever ran express passenger trains. They were 'fast goods engines' or 'mixed traffic engines'. They had little chance to excite passengers by high speed even if they had been able to produce it.

They were 'before their time' as the saying is, to the extent that lengths of existing turntables restricted design. The distance from the back of the boiler to the back of the footplate was held down to about 2 ft 8 in, so that the fireman had to have one foot on the fall-plate between engine and tender whenever he was feeding the fire.

Recurrence of design-features of this kind on locomotives on many railways engendered enginemen's common belief that designers regarded the cab as something to occupy what space was left over when every other component of engine and tender had been given all it needed.

Before any start had been made on the building of the third engine of the class, assurances had been given that the turntable restriction was to be eased; this enabled the overall length of Class S to be increased by about two feet and this was allotted entirely to the footplate and cab, which thus became one of the most commodious in Britain. (Equally large cabs had been placed

84

on Worsdell 4–4–0s but they were encumbered by splashers for the rear coupled wheels.)

When a designer advanced from eight wheels to ten, he was naturally a bit worried about how the engine would get round curves and on this account the North Eastern Class S engines were provided with flangeless tyres on the middle coupled wheels. The basic principle evidently was that the first and last coupled wheels would 'set' the engine on a sharp curve and that the side-control on the bogie should be weak enough to permit this without seriously tending to derail the bogie sideways. Flangeless tyres prevented the middle coupled wheels from interfering with this plan.

British locomotive engineers in 1899 and for a long time afterwards were extremely resistant to the scheme used in foreign countries where curvature was severe even on main lines and not merely in low-speed locations. This principle was that the locomotive should be located on a curve by its ends (just as is a bogie coach) rather than by only its rear half; this, or a good approximation to it, was achieved by applying strong side-control to the bogie and prohibiting the leading coupled wheels from resisting this, by making them flangeless. On this plan, a 4–6–0 has two pieces of rigid wheelbase and the swivelling action of the bogie accommodates the angle between them.

It seems likely that the flangeless wheels in Class S engines occasionally slipped right off the rails on very sharp curves, as flanged tyres were afterwards substituted. The probability is that the new flanges were thinner than standard and that the flanges on the leading coupled wheels were 'thinned' at the same time.

Turning now to the boiler, it may be remarked that even in the most favourable circumstances the grate area of 23.7 sq ft was not large for a 4–6–0 and in fact its potential in Class S was markedly reduced by a bad ashpan. This was very shallow over the rear axle and behind it, and there was no air-inlet at the back. So there was little chance that any Class S locomotive would ever produce any inspiring amount of power per square foot of grate area or that it would do any better at speed than a Class R.

The tops of the coupled wheels were covered by individual

splashers built out to the same overall width as the cab, but the middle ones were locally widened to clear the outer ends of the main crank-pins. All the crank-pins were out of sight when near the highest points of their revolutions and the top slide-bars were permanently hidden. It seems extraordinary that even where American example had given locomotives the best cabs in Britain, it failed to raise the running board of Class S by the few inches that would have helped enginemen and fitters very considerably. The part of the running board ahead of the cylinders had to be removed before a front cylinder-cover could be taken off. This was a noticeable feature of all North Eastern standard 2/4–6–0s and 2/4–4–2s.

Before going into regular service, No 2001 was given a try-out between Newcastle and Berwick with a heavier train of passenger vehicles than was normally run on the North Eastern. Mr. Charles Rous-Marten timed the train and published some of his figures in an article in *The Engineer* for July 21, 1899. The directly relevant part of the article began thus:

'The duty prescribed for it on this occasion was to take from Newcastle to Edinburgh, in the time allotted to the day express commonly known as the "Flying Scotsman", a train consisting of twenty-five vehicles, viz, twenty-two ordinary six wheelers, two six-wheeled brake-vans, and one observation saloon, also six wheeled, the total weight empty, exclusive of engine and tender, being 352 tons. As the engine and tender weighed no less than 105 tons—the heaviest yet seen in British practice—the total weight of engine, tender, and train amounted to 457 tons. So the task presented was no light one, although the booked running time was not specially fast, the allowance for the 124½ miles, with a stop at Berwick, being 2 h 35 min, for this represented an average travelling speed of 48.2 mph.

In spite of peremptory instructions having been given to keep the road clear for the "special", a goods train, through the blundering of some subordinate, was allowed to get in front, and this blocked the test-train so badly that it did not clear Heaton Junction, two miles from Newcastle, after several stops and slackenings, until nearly twelve minutes after the original start from the Central Station. But after once getting the road, the new locomotive went ahead bravely. It walked away with the enormous load as calmly and steadily as if this had been a normal train'.

The main task of a journalist invited to report on a test of this sort is to add to the figures that tell the story to the discerning reader some verbal comment designed to suggest to other readers that what was achieved was notable. One may notice Rous-Marten's early use of the now-familiar 'no less than' as a means of delicately telling the artless reader that he ought to gasp at what comes next. The righteous dudgeon over the 'blundering of some subordinate' recurs in Rous-Marten's writings where he reports a signal-check.

The average speed of the test-train over the $61\frac{3}{4}$ miles from leaving Heaton Junction to passing Scremerston was 48.5 mph, which was about in line with the 'Scotsman's' current booked average from Newcastle to Edinburgh, but as it represents only about 500 horsepower at the rear of the tender, it showed no outstanding ability in an engine of this size.

Mr. Rous-Marten's comment on this part of the trip was:

'This was hardly so good as had been anticipated from the excellent uphill work, but on stopping at Berwick it was ascertained that one of the excentrics had heated, the new engine being still very stiff and scarcely yet in regular working trim. This had compelled the driver to run at a comparatively slow rate on those portions of the line where the best speed is commonly made.'

(One may regret later supersession of the spelling 'excentric' by 'eccentric', the more particularly as a surprisingly large number of people pronounce the latter as 'eesentric'.)

From Berwick to Edinburgh the average speed was less than 45 mph start to stop even with allowance for a slow run-in. Mr. Rous-Marten blamed signs of overheating of the sick eccentric for restriction of speed to 65 mph even on the tempting four miles of 1 in 96 down Cockburnspath bank.

For the return journey the load was reduced to 175 tons (less than 80 per cent of that taken by 4-2-2 No 1518 on her startling test-run nine years earlier) and with that an average of 52 mph start-to-stop over 51¾ miles from New Hailes to Marshall Meadows was not dazzling even with allowance for restraint in downhill running in deference to the speed-sensitive eccentric.

There was nothing in this to persuade Gateshead that the S was going to be a 'flyer' or indeed to produce any dissent from the general British belief that something like 7 ft was the right wheel-diameter for fast running.

Later engines of Class S were built with 8¾ in diameter piston-valves (all the class got them eventually) and with narrower driving-wheel splashers, leaving space for a running board at the level of the tops of the cylinders. Below the running board was a valance extending downwards to the common level of the foot-plating ahead of the cylinders and the top of the frame of the tender. The valance had a circular-arc embayment to provide clearance for the main crank-pin. Need it have been so deep as to keep the top slide-bar out of sight? Or was this deliberate policy?

All Class S engines survived till 1928 but most of them had been taken out of service before World War II. A notable exception was No 761 (built in 1906) which was rebuilt in 1932 to act as a 'counter-pressure locomotive' for use when testing other locomotives. In this capacity No 761 was attached to the rear of a dynamometer-car itself attached to the locomotive under test. Setting No 761 in backward gear while running forward caused it to apply to the rear of the dynamometer-car a resistance that was adjustable with the aim of maintaining a pre-determined speed in spite of changes of gradient whilst the engine under test worked with fixed regulator-opening and fixed cut-off.

Much later on, the LMS developed test-cars with geared electrical generators to do the same work more elegantly and economically and so No 761 (renumbered 1699 in about 1946) became superfluous to British Railways requirements and was scrapped in about 1951.

Class S1 (2/4-6-0)

In developing the Class S1 2/4-6-0 from Class S, the 7 in increase in wheel diameter meant that the wheelbase had to be increased. The boiler barrel was also lengthened in order to reach from the front of the firebox to the more distant smokebox. The boiler had to be lifted to clear the higher wheel-tops and this made the S1 look distinctly more impressive than the S. An unnoticeable difference from the original S was the use of piston-valves in Class S1.

Apart from this, general design was the same for both classes. North Eastern tradition insisted that the running board should be at the height of the top edge of the buffer-beam and as the outside cylinders on an engine with large wheels inevitably projected above that level, the top slide-bars were rather more successfully hidden than those on Class S.

Piston-valves, $8\frac{3}{4}$ inches in diameter, in Class S1 gave it a distinct advantage in speed over Class S, which originally had flat valves, and an extra 7 in on wheel diameter was a further move in the same direction. Class S1 was in fact fast enough to run the North Eastern express trains but no more successfully than Class R 4–4–0s were doing it. The work of the smaller engines showed that there was nothing to be gained by building any more of Class S1 than the first batch of five. Why should that be? Why did not the extra size and the extra weight of Class S1 engines give them a marked advantage over the Class R 4–4–0s?

An answer, based on published information, is that the restrictive ashpan on the 4–6–0s limited the combustion-rate to something within the capacity of the smaller grate on Class R. Over 40 per cent extra adhesion weight and larger cylinders gave the bigger engine a marked advantage in getting a big train away on a steep gradient, but in only a few places was that useful in handling North Eastern express passenger trains. At that time, and indeed for more than twenty years afterwards, all the adhesion weight that any North Eastern main line passenger train engine needed to have could be placed on four wheels. So although Class S1 locomotives were used on the 'best' main line expresses for some time after they were first built, the 4–4–0s did the same work at less expense, and when larger engines were next becoming necessary, the 4–4–2 wheel arrangement was tried.

Class S2 (*2/4–6–0*)

From 1911 to 1913 Raven built a class of 'mixed traffic' 2/4–6–0 generally similar to Class S of 1899 except for

(a) a 9 in increase in boiler-diameter;

(b) the addition of a superheater, (after some early hesitation);

(c) the replacement of flat valves by piston-valves.

In their early years, these Class S2 engines were extensively employed in express passenger train service, and with loads up to about 350 tons they could run from Darlington to York in 43 minutes and could reach 75 mph on the level. Later on there were so many Class Z 'Atlantics' running that Class S2 engines were only rarely used on the fastest passenger trains, but when it did happen, a gay type of driver might surprise the interested traveller by running, even without much help from gravity, at the 'wheel-diameter speed' (mph equal to driving wheel diameter in inches) which was about as fast as any Class Z engine is known to have run on the level or indeed to have appreciably exceeded anywhere.

On the other hand, drivers knew that they were not likely to be criticized for not pushing a Class S2 engine up to the speed necessary to 'time' the fastest North Eastern trains, and most men would be content to potter along at about 60 mph with what was really a 'fast goods' engine.

In grate area, Class S2 was no bigger than Class S, first built twelve years earlier, but piston-valves and superheating gave the later engines an advantage that might show itself at the higher speeds. But Class S2 with 23.7 sq ft of grate could not be expected to compete in power output with Class Z which had 27. Class S2 was not such a large engine as its imposing appearance might suggest.

Class S3 (*3/4–6–0*)

After the end of World War I, there was a need on the North Eastern for more 'mixed traffic' locomotives and there was justification for something larger than Class S2. So a bigger boiler was needed and a higher nominal tractive effort. The former was covered by a superheater-fitted version of the boiler produced by Wilson Worsdell for his first 'Atlantic'. Larger cylinders might have covered the second point, but the three-cylinder assembly used for some years in many North Eastern locomotives had become accepted and it was reasonable to apply it in a 4–6–0 with driving wheels of 'mixed traffic' size.

In this way Class S3 came into being in 1919. Its most marked difference from Class S2 was that the three driving crank-pins were all in the leading coupled wheel-and-axle assembly. The smaller wheel-diameter was presumably chosen to obtain 30,000 lb nominal tractive effort with the $18\frac{1}{2}$ in cylinders used in the Class T3 3/0–8–0. This cylinder-block made it necessary to place the connecting rods outside the coupling rods. So far as Class S3 alone was concerned, the opposite arrangement (as used with the $16\frac{1}{2}$ in cylinder block) was permissible and preferable. It was a pity to use smaller wheels than those of Class S2, but a 'wheel-diameter speed' of 68 mph would be high enough to cover all the fast running that would normally be required of a 'mixed traffic' engine.

Thirty-eight of Class S3 were built by the North Eastern and thirty-two more by the LNER after grouping, under Gresley's direction. This is interesting in that Gresley's own comparable 'mixed traffic' engine, the K3 3/2–6–0, was being extensively multiplied at about the same time, but the K3 had a reputation for rough riding and a claim for superiority of Class S3 in that respect may have been made to justify additions to it.

Class S3 was used extensively on passenger trains but without any special distinction so far as published records go.

After 1937, the LNER rebuilt many of the class with new cylinders, running board raised above the coupled wheels and Walschaerts valve-gear for the outside cylinders. In Gresley's time, the middle valve was worked by conjugating mechanism from the outside valve-spindles; in later rebuilds, Walschaerts gear was used for all three valves.

In its rebuilt form, the S3 was a more elegant-looking locomotive with the practical advantage that the inside mechanism could be reached from below without using any inter-rail pit.

Class T and T1 (2/0–8–0)

When, near the beginning of the twentieth century, goods traffic on the North Eastern began to offer scope for engines with more than six coupled wheels, Wilson Worsdell had to consider what form an eight-coupled goods engine might take. Should it have inside cylinders or outside cylinders? Should it be a 0–8–0 or a 2–8 -0?

During the preceding twenty-five years or so, the North Eastern had never added an outside-cylinder engine to its stock apart from compound No 1619 in which the use of three cylinders had compelled two of them to be 'outside'. But an era of 'big engines' seemed to be opening and some revision of 'old Spanish customs' might be useful. Outside cylinders had the advantages:
(a) of avoiding any need for the expensive crank-axle;
(b) of leaving between the frame-plates plenty of room for access to valve gear;
(c) of leaving plenty of room for axle boxes of any reasonable width.

The only disadvantage of outside cylinders was that they placed reciprocating masses on two widely separated lines so that they had a big tendency to induce 'sway' of the engine when running fast.

For heavy pulling it was important to have as much adhesion weight as possible and therefore not to 'waste' any of the engine's weight on uncoupled wheels.

So it looked as if an outside-cylinder 0–8–0 was the thing to make for the big goods job. There would be a rather heavy overhang at the front but as no high speed would be required of the engine, this would not be specially disadvantageous.

Most of the eight-coupled locomotives in Great Britain at the time belonged to the London & North Western Railway. They were 0–8–0s and this gave an answer to one of the North Eastern designers' questions. But they had both inside cylinders and out-side cylinders and this did not answer the other question. Wilson Worsdell chose the outside-cylinder 0–8–0 and nothing happened later to question the wisdom of that choice.

There was not a lot of designing to be done in producing the

Class T 2/0–8–0. The cylinders of the Class S1 2/4–6–0s were attached to an eight-wheel chassis and a boiler not so big as that of Class S was mounted on top at a height that left room for a suitably-shaped ashpan to lie over the rear axle.

The firegrate was slightly sloped downwards towards the front, and the lower edges of the firebars were 5 in clear of the ashpan where it was 'humped' over the rear axle.

The valves were worked by direct link-motion with no offset whatever. The eccentric-rods embraced the second axle and were rather hideously cranked to clear it. Lever reversing-gear was used.

The piston valves were of the segmental type evolved by W. M. Smith but not at the time proved to the satisfaction of Wilson Worsdell, and a second batch of otherwise similar engines (Class T1) were provided with flat valves and steam reversing gear. Worsdell's decision against exclusive use of piston-valves in these engines was justified by the results of comparative tests carried out in 1906. These showed the Class T1 engine with flat valves to burn some 10 per cent less coal than did the Class T engine with piston-valves. This was opposite to the result of the similar test made some seven years earlier on Class M1 4–4–0s and may have made Worsdell wish that he had let sleeping dogs lie. There were already forty Class T engines and Worsdell decided to build no more. Further additions were made to Class T1, which numbered fifty on completion of the last batch in 1911. The old British compromise: about half of each!

As was customary on many British railways before World War I, these 0–8–0s were painted and decorated in the same manner as for passenger locomotives; each had a brass rim on its chimney, a brass ring round the boiler-barrel where it joined the smokebox and a brass casing round its safety valves. The use of less elaborate livery for goods engines than for passenger-train engines did not become a common British practice until some years later.

Class T2 (2/0–8–0)
Superheating was on the point of being accepted by the North Eastern when the last lot of Class T1 2/0–8–0s were built. By the

time the next need arose, two years later, for more big goods engines, Raven was convinced that superheating was well worth while in goods engines engaged on long hauls and so Class T2 was designed as an enlarged version of Class T plus a superheater. No matter how well flat valves worked with 'wet' steam, they had never been successful with superheated steam, and so Class T2 locomotives were provided with piston-valves. The new engine looked more powerful than Class T because the boiler (the same as that of Class S2) was 9 in fatter, and looked more business-like because economy measures had markedly reduced the amount of visible brass.

The cast-iron chimney had a wind-deflector (or *capuchon*) but no brass-rim, the boiler-barrel lagging sheet was flush with the smokebox, and the Ross 'pop' safety valves needed no casing. The height of the dome had been cut down to about half that of the chimney, giving a slightly comical appearance to the engine. The pistons had tail-rods concealed by tubular sheaths.

The first few engines had Robinson superheaters. These were of the Schmidt type with some constructional details devised by J. G. Robinson of the Great Central Railway. One feature—the attachment of elements to headers in a way that made subsequent separation awkward and laborious—was afterwards recognized to be undesirable. Each of the early Class T2 engines had a pyro-meter to indicate the temperature of the superheated steam and many a driver must have wondered whether he was supposed to allow this information to modify his way of handling the engine.

Dynamometer-car tests made with Class T2 No 1250 showed that at speeds of about 25 mph the engine could develop about 1000 horsepower at the tender drawbar when worked hard for short periods. This was in accordance with expectations from the results of elementary calculation based on the published dimen-sions of Class T2. But a suggestion that a pull exceeding the nominal tractive effort of the engine was maintained at low speed means either that there was no friction anywhere in the engine or tender, or that there was an imperfection in the dynamometer.

That Class T2 was 'successful' may be judged from the fact

that 120 engines of the class were built in eight years with only trifling departures from the original design. Like many goods engines, those of Class T2 had very long lives. In World War II, LNER men bracketed them equal to the ex-Great Central 2–8–0s in indifference to neglect, apart from the fact that if the steam reversing gear were allowed to get into poor condition it might refuse to retain any cut-off setting but that of 'full gear'. This led to low cylinder-efficiency over considerable distances and therefore waste of coal, but it did not stop the engine from working. This was what mattered when traffic was so heavy that goods engines had to be used even though in a very bad state of disrepair and had to be run for what were previously regarded as dangerously long periods between successive washouts of the boiler.

It need hardly be added that Class T2 (Q6 in LNER classification) was one of the numerous locomotive classes that were described, after 1945, as 'the engines that won the war'. That remark might have been perhaps more fittingly made about the 50 Class T1 0–8–0s that worked in France during World War I.

Class T3 (3/0–8–0)
Although by the end of World War I the North Eastern had a large number of goods engines, it had none so big as the Great Western '2800' Class and it was natural to think that a railway with so much goods and mineral traffic as the North Eastern and (in places) such steep gradients ought to have at least a few goods engines as powerful as any in the country.

The existing Class T2 was good but with a bigger boiler would be better. A bigger axle-load was permissible on most routes and the reduction of hammer blow made possible by the use of three cylinders instead of two should permit some restrictions to be raised.

So Wilson Worsdell's 5 ft 6 in boiler with 27 sq ft grate area was taken from its 1903 shelf and given a superheater and some detail modifications to be mounted on a 0–8–0 chassis with three cylinders $18\frac{1}{2} \times 26$ in with $8\frac{3}{4}$ in piston valves.

Class T3 was 17 per cent bigger than Class T2 in grate area, which is a limitation on sustained power, and about 9 per cent bigger in adhesion weight which limits the maximum tractive effort while the smooth torque of three cylinders adds another 5 or 6 per cent. On average Class T3 was bigger than Class T2 by about 15 per cent.

On Sunday August 28, 1921, Class T3 engine No 903, manned by T. C. Watson and H. Maughan of West Auckland shed, ran special tests on the North British Railway from Bridge of Earn up the Glenfarg bank of nearly six miles at 1 in 75. On the last test, the engine was worked in full gear (75 per cent cut-off) with wide-open regulator and lifted a load of 775 tons over 6.66 miles in 33 minutes. This meant development of about 760 horsepower to overcome gravity. The additional power absorbed by frictional resistance is difficult to estimate directly particularly on account of the curvature of the line and it is perhaps a pity that no dynamo-meter-car was included in the train.

Steam pressure was well maintained and it can be estimated that the indicated horsepower might be about 1200. The difference between this and 760 horsepower represents the power used in overcoming frictional resistances and it is very considerably greater than the normal expectation for goods vehicles running straight in a calm.

No figure was reported about coal-consumption, but it may be estimated that during the test the fireman was handling about a hundredweight of coal per minute.

Classes V and V1 (2/4-4-2)

Class R 4-4-0s were handling North Eastern express trains very well at the beginning of the twentieth century but Worsdell had realized that something bigger was going to be needed before very long. He had in fact produced the Class S 2/4-6-0 and, because this was no 'flyer', had gone on to make the larger-wheeled Class S1 which was better than Class S but not better than Class R. One of the defects of Class S1 was the restricted space between the firebars and the ashpan where it was humped over the rear axle.

The Great Northern had tried some 'Atlantics' and in 1902 brought out a bigger one with a wide firebox and a 5 ft 6 in

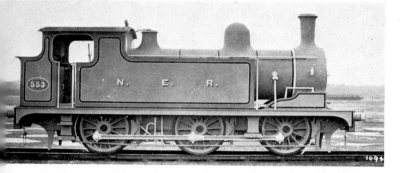

No 1326 (Class I). Note Joy valve-gear.
No 1517 (Class J). Large sand-boxes (cf. Class I). Outside steam-chest.
Smokebox oddly deformed by unusual positions of cylinders (see Fig. 6)
No 553 (Class L). Joy valve-gear. Extra blocks on buffer beams.
No 1638 (Class M1). Extended smokebox. Outside steam-chest.

22. No 1783 Class (O). Westinghouse brake-cylinder very prominent. Note bogie wheels with twelve spokes

23. No 1897 (Class P). Note cab-roof ventilator open behind the whistles

24. No 1678 (Class P2). Huge safety-valve cover. Smokebox flat and short

25. No 2338 (Class P3). Raised wind-deflector on chimney. Pyrometer lead from superheater just behind chimney. Mechanical lubricator. Pop safety valves

boiler. Was this a line for the North Eastern to try? The wide firebox was a new venture in Britain and might be troublesome. But even without it, the low rear axle of an 'Atlantic' allowed the ashpan to be lower than it could be in a 4–6–0 with big driving wheels, and so an 'Atlantic', even with a narrow firebox might be worth trying.

The increase in grate area from 20.5 sq ft in Class R to 23.7 sq ft in Class S1 had not effected much increase in power, so something bigger still was needed. Churchward on the Great Western had a 4–6–0 with about 27 sq ft of grate; the North Eastern ought not to be satisfied with anything less. And if the Great Northern could use a 5 ft 6 in boiler, so could the North Eastern. The Class S1 4–6–0s had cylinders 20 in by 26 in and something a bit bigger was appropriate for the 'Atlantic'. Nobody in Britain seemed to like going above 20 inches in diameter and Churchward was using 30 in stroke. So a safe compromise was 20 by 28. W. M. Smith's piston valves seemed to be working quite well and so it might be sensible to use them in a new design.

Thoughts on these lines may well have led to Worsdell's Class V 'Atlantic' No 532, built in 1903. It represented the classic definition of a locomotive as an 'engine on a carriage' with the major dimensions listed above. The general 'styling' was that established on the North Eastern by T. W. Worsdell and no imagination was required in covering that aspect of design. Whether anyone thought that No 532 was beautiful or not depended very much on his predilections and affections. She certainly lacked the external crudity of the first Churchward 4–6–0s and was 'neat' in the Victorian sense, but the narrow smokebox made her look very flat-chested and the large brass casing round the safety valves escaped—if it did escape—from being classed as 'gross' by only a narrow margin.

At least in respect of outward appearance it is a pity that Worsdell did not adopt the extended smokebox as applied by Ivatt to the Great Northern 'large Atlantic'. It was also a pity that he *did* copy that design in keeping the cab-roof close to the top of the boiler and well below the top of the safety valves as this left room for only shallow front look-outs in the front sheet of the cab. They were deep enough for the men to be able to see all that they needed to see if they did not mind pressing their heads on the roof. But complaints were evidently made and so the cab-roofs of the second and subsequent engines were more highly arched and this left room for larger look-outs.

Ten Class V locomotives were built in 1903 and 1904 and were set to work on the 'best' North Eastern trains. They were big noisy engines. As was the case with most of the bigger British locomotives of the period, the valves were not big enough to enable the full output of the boiler to be fed to the cylinders at an economical cut-off at normal running speeds, and the smoke-box layout was far from ideal. Consequently Class V engines were not light on coal and were not 'free-running'. This means that they could be made to go fast only at late cut-off because only in that condition were the port-openings for admission of steam to the cylinders large enough for steam to get into the cylinders fast enough. The engines punched their way along by wasteful force rather than by flowing finesse. They *could* beat Class R engines but rarely did so. This is not in itself a criticism of Class V or of anyone if the engine 'keeps time'. Nor is a driver's disinclination to work an engine any harder than is necessary to keep time a cause for criticism even if the train is running late. So the failure of Class V to show anything very sparkling in ordinary service should not be taken as a reason for suggesting that Worsdell or anyone in his department ought to have done better than this.

In the *Locomotive Magazine* for April 14, 1906 is an account of a run by Class V No 784 which took a train of ten bogie coaches and two others of unspecified type from Darlington to York in 45 minutes. A maximum speed of 79 mph is said to have been attained somewhere south of Northallerton, but this is hard to believe as the average from the start to Thirsk was 57 mph, from there to Alne 60 mph, and from Alne to a stop just short of York station was $60\frac{1}{2}$ mph. Comparison of the times with those of other runs suggests a maximum speed not higher than 64 mph.

By the year 1910, North Eastern designers had had the benefit of much more experience with piston valves than was available at Gateshead in 1903 and a modified form of Class V, known as Class Vi, was built in 1910. The appearance of the front of the engine was improved by some extension of the smokebox (more would have been better) and the top edges of the frame-plates dipped to the buffer-beam in a bold arc, convex on top, instead of the modest concavity of the 1903 design. The driving wheel splashers were narrow and each coupling-rod in its high positions was hidden by a valance under a raised running-board which extended from the cylinder to the cab with a couple of waves to clear the crank-pin oil-boxes.

There was no significant change in any published dimension and so the unofficial observer was given no reason to expect a Vi to be any better than a V on the road. Indeed Table 1, derived from examination of published records, shows quite the reverse, but the Vi may well have benefited from elimination of detail-defects unrecognizable by anyone not directly concerned in the daily performance of the engines. Had not the three-cylinder Class Z appeared soon after Class Vi and captivated everyone with its smooth and lively running, Class Vi might well have been multiplied to become the North Eastern's 'crack' express locomotive.

Two-cylinder engines, at least when somewhat run-down, rode so roughly and subjected the frame and the enginemen to such vibration that a three-cylinder engine was inevitably more attractive for fast-running. Many years later, when ease of maintenance of locomotives became paramount, such attraction had to be sternly resisted, but in 1911 a bit of complication under the boiler did not worry anyone very much and so the three-cylinder engine could win the day.

In the *Railway Magazine* for August 1924, Mr. C. J. Allen reported ten runs from Darlington to York behind an engine of Class S2, two of Class V, two of Class Vi and five of Class Z in trains weighing from 340 to 395 tons. The two shortest net times of 44.2 minutes and 44.8 minutes were returned by Class Vi No 699 with 340 tons and Class Vi No 698 with 350 tons. The former averaged 70 mph from Otterington to Beningbrough and the next best average over this length was 68.7 mph by a similarly loaded Class Z engine No 2208. No 699 also attained the highest top speed (75 mph) of any and the next best was 74 mph by Class S2 No 798 with 350 tons in achieving a net time of 45.8 minutes for the 44.1 miles.

These figures are interesting because they show that the North Eastern lesser lights, which tended to be outshone by the numerical superiority of Class Z and its preferential use on the best trains, were not essentially much inferior to it when occasion arose for smart running. But it was natural for enginemen to prefer a Z to a V because two big pistons thumping the fourth axle on the engine were bound to shake the men harder than three little pistons doing smooth work on the third axle.

Classes W and W1   (4–6–0T and 4–6–2T)
The Scarborough–Whitby section of the North Eastern was one of the railways to which the name 'Fred Karno's line' was colloquially applied. (Fred Karno was the leader of the troupe of comics in which Charles Chaplin graduated.)

The passenger from Scarborough to Whitby had first to walk the full length of a longish platform to find his train in a bay, still further out. After only a few hundred yards' propulsion by the engine, the train started its real journey by moving back towards the station before entering Falsgrave tunnel as the preliminary to a bit of railway mountaineering. For the first five miles the grades are ordinary but the next $2\frac{1}{2}$ miles are markedly adverse and the remaining $2\frac{1}{2}$ to Ravenscar station at the very summit are continuously upwards at around 1 in 40. But even that is flat compared with the cross slope of the country as the shortest route to sea level from Ravenscar is about $\frac{1}{4}$ mile down 1 in 2.

The descent on the railway for $3\frac{1}{2}$ miles northwards from Ravenscar is about as steep as the ascent from Scarborough. Beyond the bottom of the dip near Robin Hood's Bay a half-size repetition of the Ravenscar 'hump' has to be surmounted before the train, after much braking, reaches Whitby West Cliff station. This, however, is not really Whitby, and so the engine used to run round the train to start it back towards Scarborough before diverging to the left at Prospect Hill Junction. Then brake power was required to make sure that the train came to a smooth stop in Whitby Town and not to a rough one in Whitby town.

The Scarborough–Whitby line was clearly no speedway and few trains beat an average of 18 mph from starting at Scarborough to stopping at Whitby Town.

Steep gradients on any line may give the impression that they meant very hard work by the engines. There is, however, no essential connection between the two things. Loads are (prudently) restricted to what the engine can re-start on the steepest gradient in reasonable conditions, and scheduled times are adjusted so that the engines need not work any harder than they normally do anywhere else. They have to pull hard on the steep patches but at such low speed that the power output is low. Coal consumption per unit of work done on the train tends to be high because the train is lighter than usual in relation to the engine.

For the enginemen, unusually steep gradients make it more important to keep the sanding gear in working order and the boiler pressure not too far below the rated maximum.

When you found that 0–4–4 tank engines had not enough adhesion weight to be sure of coping with steep gradients, you at once thought of trying a six-coupled engine. This happened on the North Eastern in connection with the line between Scarborough, Whitby and Saltburn, where heavy loads and slippery rails could make the working of 0–4–4 tank engines of Class O very unreliable. By the year 1906 this was becoming a serious matter.

The 0–6–2Ts of Classes B1 and N would have had a distinct advantage in their adhesion weight of 45 tons as against 30 tons because this would make them less likely to 'stall' in difficult conditions. They had, however, no advantage in boiler power and this may have persuaded Wilson Worsdell that a bigger six-coupled tank than the Class B1 was required to provide a clear-cut solution to the haulage problem.

A six-coupled tank engine might take various forms. The 0–6–0T had the advantage that all its weight was on the coupled wheels, but the disadvantage that its adhesion weight with nearly empty tanks was markedly less than it was when the tanks were full. Moreover, with no guiding wheels, it tended to wear rails and wheel-flanges noticeably if used on curved track at speed. No high speed was possible on the Scarborough–Whitby route because of the sharpness of the curves, but that in itself suggested the desirability of using locomotives with guiding wheels. And as nobody wanted the bother of turning engines round at the ends of short journeys, a 'double-end' wheel arrangement might have suggested itself to Worsdell the more especially as his friend Churchward on the Great Western had by 1906 shown himself to be strongly in favour of the 2/2–6–2T wheel-arrangement. But there was no tradition of outside cylinders for tank engines on the North Eastern, and indeed clearances on the Scarborough–Whitby line may well have been too fine to permit the use of any tank engine with any combination of wheel diameter and cylinder-diameter that would do what was wanted.

The next obvious alternative was a 2–6–2T with inside cylinders. Only the Lancashire & Yorkshire had any engine of this description. Early experience with this Hoy design was unhappy and later experience was even worse. Information about this may have deflected Worsdell from a 2–6–2T but it is hard to understand what made him adopt the 4–6–0T unless indeed he had the intention that engines of this type should not normally run bunker first. W. M. Smith had died in 1906 or he might well have dissuaded Worsdell from what must be regarded as an indiscretion. But he was quite confident in his own judgment (or somebody else's) as a batch of ten 4–6–0Ts were built in 1907–8 without awaiting service results from two or three before deciding whether they were worth multiplying. The design and building were indeed completed before certain bridges on the coast line had been strengthened to take the new engines and so some of them were first used in the Leeds–Harrogate–Wetherby area.

The first five of these engines had markedly extended smokeboxes. This gave the front end a massively powerful look, but the short bunker behind the cab made the rear end seem unnaturally 'chopped-off'. The nickname 'Willies' given by enginemen to Class W somehow matched their odd appearance. They did not look right and in fact they were not right in that they could not carry enough coal to keep them going as hard as they might for a good day's work. So between May 1915 and January 1917, the ten of them were extended into 4–6–2Ts with bunkers that could hold 4 tons of coal instead of the original 2¼ tons. Against this advantage had to be set the disadvantages that the total weight of the locomotive was increased by 9 tons whilst the adhesion weight was reduced by 4 tons.

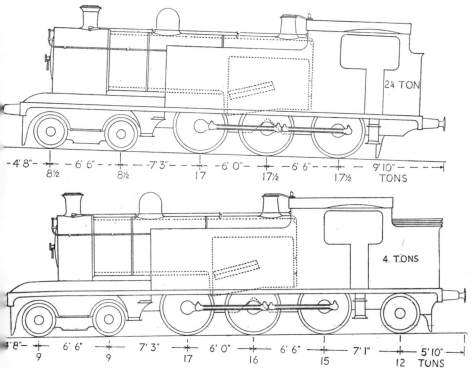

Fig. 5 A 'Willy' and a 'Woolly Willy' in characteristic attitudes on the 'Fred Karno's line' between Scarborough and Whitby

Owing to the longer and shallower firebox, the W and W1 classes were not so easy to fire as the 0–4–4Ts of Class O. In Class W the distance of over 7 ft from the coal to the fire-hole at least left room to swing a cat in, but was perhaps greater than the average fireman's ideal.

With the usual four-coach train weighing about 87 tons, even a Class O engine fully supplied with coal and water constituted 37 per cent of the total moving mass. With a W1, the figure was 47 per cent. This emphasizes that the low-power weight ratio of a steam locomotive makes it an inefficient tractive agent on steep gradients.

Class W were the first North Eastern engines to be fitted with blast-pipes specially designed and made to be variable in effective cross-section. The blast-pipe proper stood inside another pipe and exhaust steam normally came out of both. Steam could be kept out of the outer pipe by closing a butterfly-valve whereupon concentration of the exhaust in the inner pipe gave the steam-jet a higher speed and therefore a stronger suction.

Prominent features of the 'Willies' in their original form were the tall brass trumpet containing Ramsbottom type safety-valves, the blower valve operating spindle extending from cab to smoke-box about 10 in above the boiler lagging plates and a 6 in copper pipe reaching across the frame, underneath the boiler-barrel, to connect the side-tanks at their front ends. As was common in Wilson Worsdell's practice, the side-tanks were very tall, so much so indeed that in later years, each engine was fitted with a steel stay, of circular arc form and ⊥-section reaching over the boiler to enable each tank to get a bit of support from the other.

But in neither form did Class W engines completely displace the 0-4-4 tank engines from the Scarborough-Saltburn route and indeed as late as 1920 the latter were still the predominant class there.

In the late 1930s, the W1s were largely displaced from their original job by Gresley's 4-6-2T rebuilds (LNER class A8) of the North Eastern Class D 4-4-4Ts and the W1s were scattered to a number of sheds in the southern part of the North Eastern system.

In 1938, the writer observed one of the W1s to reach 60 mph with a passenger train between Pickering and Malton, and this was a slightly surprising speed for a 'Woolly Willy'. On arrival at Malton he noticed an inspection-door in front of the smokebox to be open and he was able to see that one of the piston tail-rods had been running without oil. This was an unusual circumstance in those days, but worse things happened to engines in World War II. After the war, most of the WIs were given light duties in different North Eastern areas and they all continued in service for a total of about forty years each.

Class X (3/4-8-0T)

In 1908 Robinson on the Great Central had produced a three-cylinder 0-8-4 tank engine for hump-pushing at the new coal-concentration yard at Wath near Barnsley. As the North Eastern was at that time completing near Middlesbrough similar sorting sidings (named 'Erimus', the resolute Latin motto of the town of Middlesbrough), it naturally occurred to someone that a specialized type of locomotive might be useful there. As a three-cylinder engine receives six piston-impulses per revolution of the driving-wheels, it might be presumed to be less likely to 'stall' when pushing slowly than was a two-cylinder engine. Eight-coupled wheels were certainly necessary to take adhesion weight adequate for hard pushing; for the engine to have a reasonably large bunker, it seemed that two additional axles would be necessary. So the wheel-arrangement might be 0-8-4 or 2-8-2 or 4-8-0. If the first-named were adopted, the engine would be bound to look very like the Great Central giant. The second arrangement is 'double-ended' which might be advantageous, but any non-driving axle behind the coupled wheels has a tendency to take weight off them when the engine is pulling (or pushing) hard in the forward direction.

So the 3/4-8-0 scheme was adopted, and this placed the driving wheels at the back end, which gave them maximum adhesion weight when the engine was working chimney-first. For this reason, the Great Central 3/0-8-4Ts were preferably worked bunker-first. In actual practice, tank engines working over short distances were normally set with smokebox facing the natural wind, so that coal-dust from the bunker was less likely to be blown on to the enginemen. To them this was more important than weight-transfer between the axles.

In the North Eastern Class X, the inside piston drove a crank in the leading coupled axle, and the outside pistons ought to have driven cranks in the leading coupled wheels. Why they were given long piston-rods and long connecting rods to drive cranks in the second pair of coupled wheels is not at all obvious; nothing so irrational was done in any other North Eastern three-cylinder design. It almost looks as if the designers were so unsure of themselves on this new ground that they felt safer in copying Robinson's 'divided drive' than in thinking carefully on the subject. Robinson had no choice on this point, because his was the 0–8–4 wheel-arrangement; the 4–8–0 had no such restriction. Gateshead deliberately accepted the disadvantage that the valves for the outside cylinders were driven by eccentrics on an axle different from the one driven by the outside pistons. In normal service this would not matter, but breakage of an intermediate coupling-rod would put the engine right out of action. Perhaps this was not regarded as very important in an engine that would not normally go far from home.

The inside valve, above the cylinder and parallel to it, was driven by link motion through rocking levers and a short rocking shaft, designed to provide the appropriate 'rise' and 'offset'. Each crosshead was guided by a single slide-bar above it. The packing of six eccentrics and a crank on the leading coupled axle was not new to the North Eastern as it had already been done on the 3C/4–4–0 No 1619, but neither fitters nor enginemen could have liked it very much. If they did not, the coming of No 1350 was an evil day for them as this feature of her construction was repeated in all of the numerous three-cylinder engines afterwards built for the North Eastern. Thence the three-cylinder system spread to the Great Northern Railway and its application was expanded with great effect by Gresley on the LNER. Thus an artifice adopted by Robinson to help locomotives to run slowly eventually became a characteristic of the fastest locomotives in Great Britain. Wilson Worsdell provided the first link in the chain of design connecting the extremes.

At Erimus yard, each Class X tank engine was normally on duty for a spell of 24 hours before returning to the shed. As the coal-capacity of the bunker was only just over 4 tons, it is clear that the firemen's work was nothing like so hard as it normally was in main line service even in 1909.

Class X engines, like the Robinson 'Wath tanks' worked regularly for forty years. In their later days, a black 'Humpy' standing cold, dirty and neglected in a dark, unkempt running shed, was a melancholy contrast with the sparkling, gaily-painted green-and-gold giant that toyed with trains of fifty loaded wagons on the newly-raised humps of Erimus.

Class Y (3/4–6–2T)

The success of the Class X 'Humpies' suggested the possible value of a tank engine of about the same size for taking goods trains over short distances. It would need to be able to run bunker-first at reasonably high speed and this naturally suggested the provision of controlled side-movement for the axle at the bunker end of the engine. A slight re-arrangement of Class X produced a 3/4–6–2T of somewhat longer wheelbase. Thus was evolved Class Y, in the same general style as Class X but with boiler-barrel 9 in fatter. The grate area of 23.7 sq ft was common to both types.

After their first venture, pardonably cautious, into three-cylinder propulsion, the North Eastern designers became bolder and in Class Y placed all three main driving crank-pins in the leading driving-wheel-and-axle assembly. This scheme was used exclusively in all later North Eastern three-cylinder designs in conjunction with casting all three cylinders and steam-chests in one piece. This means a rather complicated casting but with the advantage of minimizing the number of joints where steam might leak. It had the disadvantage, however, that damage to an outside cylinder (low-speed collisions in and near engine sheds did this more frequently than one might imagine) might easily mean scrapping the whole cylinder-block. On the other hand it must be mentioned that the outside cylinders of Classes Y, Z and D drove connecting rods placed between the wheel-boss and the coupling rod; the cylinders were therefore tucked closely up to the frame-plates and so were less likely to be struck in a side-long collision than were outside cylinders in the normal position.

The general arrangement of cylinders, valves and valve-gear in Class Y was as in Class X, but as the volume swept by the $16\frac{1}{2}$ in pistons of Class Y was some 16 per cent less than that of Class X there was a justification for adopting piston-valves of $7\frac{1}{2}$ in diameter instead of the $8\frac{3}{4}$ in valves of the earlier engine.

Twenty Class Y engines were built as the initial batch and no addition was ever made to this number. There would seem to have been so much scope for short-distance goods engines in the industrial part of the North Eastern system between the Tees and the Tyne as to suggest useful employment for more than this number of tank engines of this size. It is easily overlooked, however, that in an engine for handling loose-coupled goods trains, brake-power is as important as pulling power. Class Y, for example, had only 56 tons on the braked wheels, whereas a Class P3 0–6–0 with tender had a total of 88 tons. It was a nuisance to pull a big tender about on short hauls but its extra brake power gave a driver confidence to bring a big goods train more quickly down a bank than he would have dared with the smaller brake-power of a tank engine.

Rather remarkably, Class Y engines running on flat or easily graded lines were rated as equal to the eight-coupled engines of Classes T, T1 and T2. Between York and Darlington, for example, the maximum allowable load in a 'C' goods train (averaging 20 mph) was 1000 tons of empty vehicles or 1215 tons of loaded vehicles. For 'B' goods trains averaging 25 mph the corresponding figures were 900 and 1000.

So Class Y hauled its heaviest trains on the flatter parts of the North Eastern Railway, although half of them normally worked in Durham. Its lighter duties were undertaken in a variety of places and the writer was interested to see one of the class shunting at Boroughbridge on that other-worldly line from Pilmoor to Knaresborough.

Class Z (3/4–4–2)

When Vincent Raven came to the North Eastern locomotive throne in 1910, he probably had the usual intention of anyone at such a juncture to produce a new design of main line passenger train locomotive that should look impressive and should be superior to any already on the line. Raven was in a slightly better position to do this than others may have been because the North Eastern 'big engines' had not been brilliant.

Wilson Worsdell's 'winner' was the Class R 4-4-0. His Class V 'Atlantics' were neither light on coal nor spritely. The four-cylinder compound 'Atlantics', like most compounds, could be light on coal when everything was in their favour, but were not marvellous 'flyers'. The Class R1 4-4-0 was not far short of a 'flop'. A three-cylinder 'Atlantic' would not be quite so complicated as the four-cylinder compounds and not quite so well balanced at speed, but it need not have the heavy axle-thumps of a partly run-down Class V.

Three-cylinder propulsion had first been adopted by the North Eastern because it gave a smoother torque than was possible in any engine with cranks at right angles. Where three-cylinders drove on to a common axle, the horizontal loads on the axle-boxes were small and the reciprocating parts could be balanced satisfactorily by quite small weights in the wheels. Three cylinders could in fact give smooth torque and smooth running. As the latter commended itself specially in respect of fast-running engines, it looked as if it would be a valuable feature in a new 'Atlantic'.

Robinson on the Great Central had built an 'Atlantic' so equipped; it was still in service in 1910 but no more had been built like it. This was hardly an encouragement to the North Eastern to go in for three-cylinder 'Atlantics' but nevertheless they did it, and moreover, twenty engines of an untried design were ordered from the North British Locomotive Company. As there still persisted in some North Eastern minds a question about the all-round utility of superheating, ten of the engines were built with superheaters and ten without. The first group was classed as Z1 and the other as Z, but when all had received super-heaters later on, the class designation was altered from Z1 to Z just for a change. The dimensions tabulated in this book refer to the superheater-fitted version; the 'wet' steam engines had $15\frac{1}{2}$ in cylinders.

The general layout of Class Z was that of the four-cylinder compound 'Atlantics' but the boiler was that of Class Vi. The grate was slightly sloped throughout its length, the ashpan was arched over the rear axle and air could be admitted to the ashpan at back and front.

Half-way between the tube-plates was a vertical plate perforated to admit the fire-tubes. The feed-water was injected into the boiler ahead of this plate and was heated by the front halves of the fire-tubes before seeping back to the rear part of the boiler where the real boiling was done.

The blast-pipe was normal but it was surrounded by a co-axial truncated cone with a radial clearance of about $1\frac{1}{2}$ inches. The bottom of the cone was a few inches above the floor of the smoke-box. The action of the blast induced a vacuum in the space between the cone and the blast-pipe and this lifted any small 'char' from the vicinity of the foot of the blast-pipe into the chimney whence it first rose into the air and then fell on to the ground or on to the train. This was the char-ejector applied to earlier North Eastern engines with the object of prohibiting any deep accumulation of char in the smokebox. (See Class Y smokebox, Fig 3, p 68).

A short petticoat-pipe was mounted just below the main petticoat-pipe which was double-walled. Steam from the small ejector was discharged into the inter-wall space whence it escaped through a hole at the top.

Over the bogie, in line abreast across the engine, lay the three cylinders. Between them were two $7\frac{1}{2}$ in piston-valves, one for each outside cylinder; above the inside cylinder was its valve, inclined downwards from front to back so that its axis intersected that of the driving axle. Stephenson-type valve-gear worked each 'outside' valve directly; similar gear worked the inside valve with a lateral offset of about 8 inches.

The ratio of valve-size to cylinder-volume was higher than that in any other North Eastern main-line engine and this gave Class Z a touch of speed that the others lacked. Whether this was a deliberate intention of the designer cannot now be ascertained. Perhaps it was. Or perhaps he simply used the design of valve already applied to Class Y. But whether by design or accident, the best speed range for valve-performance and the best speed range for cylinder-efficiency at a brisk combustion-rate over-lapped between 67 and 84 mph, whereas the Class V1 two cylinder 'Atlantics' on the North Eastern had 50 to 55 mph as the corresponding range.

The coupled-wheel splashers and the coupling-rod splashers of Class V1 were virtually repeated in Class Z. With the connecting-rod between the wheel-boss and the coupling-rod, each outside cylinder was set so well in that it did not interrupt the valance under the running-board and was an unobtrusive feature of the engine. Bedecked in green and gold, a Class Z 'Atlantic' was a magnificent embodiment of Edwardian ideas on the outward appearance of steam locomotives. All the lines of the engine suggested majesty, grace, power and speed. One might carp at the narrow brass rim on the short chimney, and suggest that the engine was rather a big girl to be wearing such a little hat. At the other end of the boiler, the fat brass casing for the four safety-valves was perhaps a little *too* fat to please everyone. Perhaps someone actually made such remarks to Raven. Certainly the later members of Class Z had plain cast-iron chimneys and two Ross 'pop' safety-valves on each engine. Form and colour combined to make a Class Z engine a picture of taste and dignity. (But a contemporary all-black North Western 'Claughton' was no less impressive.)

Perhaps the most notable feat of a Class Z locomotive in load-pulling at speed was that of No 732 in taking 545 tons from York to Darlington in 50 min 15 sec start to stop. (*Railway Magazine* June 1912.)

No 2163, hauling 220 tons, averaged $77\frac{1}{2}$ mph over 23.4 miles, slightly falling from Otterington to Skelton Bridge, and averaged $81\frac{1}{2}$ mph over the last ten miles, which are level. This happened in 1923 when 'eighty on the level' was a rare occurrence in Great Britain.

The early performance of Class Z in service showed that here was the desired super-Class R. Superheaters were fitted to the ten 'wet steam' engines and in seven years (including the four of

World War I), the stock of Class Z engines had been increased to fifty. This design was the climax of development of North Eastern steam. It was as much the last word in excellence as its designation was the last letter in the alphabet.

Class D (1913) (3/4-4-4T)

The Class O 0-4-4 tank engines (LNER G5) were among the best of their size to run anywhere but some duties in the Newcastle, Saltburn, Northallerton, Bishop Auckland area tended to overtax them and so there arose a need for a larger size of tank-engine able to run at a mile a minute in each direction. To meet a need for more power on the Whitby–Scarborough line, six-coupled tank engines had been developed with dubious success. The need in Durham was for more power and speed rather than for better rail-grip. This in conjunction with enthusiasm for three-cylinder propulsion suggested that there might be no need to go beyond four-coupling. The desirability of a 'double-end' wheel arrangement for two-way tank engines is superficially obvious and so thoughts naturally turned to 2-4-2T or 4-4-4T. The former, however, could hardly have been made big enough to meet the demand for more power than a 0-4-4T could provide and so the North Eastern chose a three-cylinder 4-4-4T.

This wheel arrangement had never been widely used in Great Britain, and indeed, as it can transmit power through only two axles out of six, it looked uneconomical in that it did not use much of the engine's weight for the vital purpose of adhesion. The smooth torque from three cylinders would certainly make rather more use of any given adhesion weight than was possible with two cylinders, but the difference is not great.

Nevertheless, Raven took the plunge and produced a very handsome tank engine entirely in the T. W. Worsdell style of external form except, of course, for the outside cylinders, which he never used. In one respect the appearance was improved by what might almost be described as cheating. The radial distance from the boiler-barrel lagging plates to the barrel itself was about $5\frac{1}{2}$ in, which is about twice as much as usual so that the 'boiler'

26. No 1927 (Class Q). Clerestory cab-roof
27. No 1870 (Class Q1). Largest coupled wheels in Britain. Brass ring round
    boiler at rear of smokebox. Clerestory cab-roof
28. No 1026 (Class R). Extended smokebox. Superheater
29. No 1238 (Class R1). Westinghouse pump just visible near smokebox on
    opposite side of engine

30. No 2003 (Class S). Cylinder projecting above running-board. Small splasher for big end of connecting-rod. Wavy reversing rod. Brass-rimmed chimney

31. No 754 (Class S). Note difference from No 2003 in running-board and splashers. Chimney with wind-deflector and brass rim.

32. No 2111 (Class S1). Tall safety-valve cover

33. No 797 (Class S2). Pyrometer lead from superheater in smokebox. Raised running-board with valance.

looked fatter than it really was, and the smokebox was enlarged
to match, A flanged make-up pipe, 5 in high, was placed between
each safety-valve column and the seating on the top of the outer
firebox. It is interesting to note to what lengths designers would
sometimes go in order to make their engines look more agreeable
to them. They could only hope that no observer would find them
offensive to the eye as there is no certain way of anticipating taste
or accounting for it.

As the class-letter of the three-cylinder 'Atlantics' built in 1911
was the last letter in the alphabet, the new tank engine was given
the letter D, first used in 1886 for two C/2–4–0s and disused after
they were rebuilt as 4–4–0s of Class F1.

Prominent on the right hand side of the Class D 3/4–4–4Ts
were the Westinghouse pump alongside the smokebox and the
steam reversing gear just behind it at the top of the frame-plate.
The reversing gear itself was beautifully accessible in this position
but it restricted top-side access to the valve-gear closely packed
between the frame-plates exactly as in the Class Z 'Atlantics'.
With need for access in mind, it is impossible wholly to admire
the North Eastern three-cylinder system, but, bound by British
convention, the designer had no real alternative. Gresley's rebuilding of a North Eastern S3 in 1937 showed what could be
done, but nothing but a trial of the uniflow system ever persuaded the North Eastern to use outside valve-gear.

Although the designation of the wheel arrangement was symmetrical, the dimensions of the wheelbase of Class D were not so.
This may have been deliberate as there was a tradition that an
exactly symmetrical wheelbase made an engine more likely to
build up bad sway about a vertical axis than if there were some
asymmetry in it.

That Class D was 'successful' may be judged from the fact that
forty-five of them were built in eight years, including the four
years of World War I and three commercially uncertain years
immediately after it. On the other hand, an initial announcement
that they were intended to work over Stainmore summit to
Tebay was not fulfilled beyond a short experimental period and
in view of the very steep gradients of that line this is not surprising.

A 4-4-4T is not a distinguished rail-gripper. That something better might have been done is suggested by Gresley's re-building of the engines to the 3/4-6-2T arrangement in 1931 to 1936, although it is fair to add that some of the duties of the class became more difficult in the 1930s than they were twenty years earlier.

In the *Railway Magazine* for July 1914, Mr. C. J. Allen recorded that Class D No 2145 took 130 tons from York to Thirsk, 22.2 miles in $25\frac{1}{2}$ minutes start to stop, with a top speed of $62\frac{1}{2}$ mph. From Thirsk the train passed Northallerton at low speed in $10\frac{1}{2}$ minutes and stopped at Eaglescliffe (22.2 miles) in just over 27 minutes, having touched 71.4 mph down 1 in 170.

Class 4-6-2 (3/4-6-2)

Of British railway staff, the higher officials at least could not have been very happy after World War I, when rumours arose of amalgamation of railways or of nationalization of railways. The North Western and the Lancashire & Yorkshire had amalgamated at the end of 1921, and soon afterwards it became clear that the railways of Britain were to be arranged in 'groups' at the end of 1922. In each such group, one company was likely to be dominant and it would be useful for any railway man to be a member of that company. So it was important to do anything that might impress whatever powers that were, or would be, that one's own railway was better than the others.

In what might have been surmised to be an 'East Coast' group, the North Eastern was a larger company than the Great Northern but the latter, by the fact of having headquarters in London, already had its figurative foot in the door of any new organization that would certainly be centred in that city.

The North Eastern had a good solid locomotive stock, but with nothing newly dramatic or glamorous, whereas the Great Northern was strongly suspected of working on a 'Pacific' design during the year 1921. Early in 1922 this was known for certain, and so the North Eastern had clearly to get moving pretty quickly on something equally striking and this could be nothing less than a 'Pacific'. Prestige demanded that at least one such engine should be running before the end of 1922 and this left absolutely no time for elaborate cogitation. The mere step in size from 'Atlantic' to 'Pacific' would bring problems of its own; there was no time to cope with additional problems likely to arise from any departure from design principles tested and proved by the North Eastern itself. So the new 'Pacific' had to be an extended Class Z 'Atlantic'.

Fourteen years earlier the Great Western had developed a 'Pacific' in exactly that way from its standard 'Star' and the result had not been very successful. This was not encouraging but nevertheless limitation of time left the North Eastern with no option but to try the same procedure and hope for the best.

The first Great Northern 'Pacific' was running in April 1922 and the first rejoinder that the North Eastern could make was to release to the press a diagram of the 'Pacific' that was beginning to take shape at Darlington. Such a diagram was published in the *Railway Magazine* for July 1922 in convenient proximity to similar diagrams for the Great Western 'Pacific' and the Great Northern 'Pacific'. Such a preview of a forthcoming class of locomotive was unusual, but not unprecedented. Ten years earlier, the *Locomotive Magazine* had published a shaded sectional drawing of the Great Central 4–6–0 *Sir Sam Fay* some time before the engine started to run.

In proceeding from ten wheels to twelve, a locomotive designer was inevitably concerned with possible difficulties in getting the longer engine round curves. The North Eastern three-cylinder layout required the distance between the bogie-centre and the leading coupled axle to be greater than it was in the Great Western and Great Northern 'Pacifics' and so the coming North Eastern 'Pacific' would be likely to have a longer wheelbase than either of them. Darlington coped with this but was ill-advised to depart from its own practice in 'Atlantics' by providing the rear axle with axleboxes between the wheels instead of outside them. This was a weak point in the Great Western 'Pacifics' and it was a feature that had been tried and rejected by a number of American users of 'Pacifics'. Experience with the earlier North Eastern 'Pacifics' led to the adoption of outside axleboxes for the rear axles of the last two and all eventually had that feature.

In contrast to the considerable difference in external appearance between the North Eastern and Great Northern 'Pacifics', their significant dimensions in respect of power and speed differed only slightly. In pulling, running, and burning coal per unit of work done, little difference was to be expected between the two classes of locomotive and there has been no suggestion that the comparative tests made in 1923 showed any great difference. In neither design were the valves so large as they might usefully have been and the deficiency was almost exactly the same for both. In their original form the Gresley 'Pacifics' were heavy on coal, and the Raven engines were about equally so.

On accessibility of mechanism the Gresley engine was much the better; it had no valve-gear whatever under the boiler whereas all the valve-gear of the Raven engine was packed between the frame-plates and between the cylinder-block and the leading coupled axle. This much could be distinguished simply by looking at the engines, but other aspects of maintenance, more important because of their number, could be assessed only by comparing large groups of engines employed on a wide range of duties over many years. In other words it simply could not be done in time to influence the decision as to which design (if either) was to be adopted as a standard by the LNER.

In regular service the North Eastern 'Pacifics' were normally kept on the main line between York and Edinburgh and the only possible yardstick of their efforts was comparison with those of the Class Z 'Atlantics'. As no more was demanded (at least officially) of the 'Pacifics' than what the 'Atlantics' were doing, it was perhaps to be expected that only on rare occasions would the former produce power commensurate with their size; certainly this turned out to be the case.

As the Raven 'Pacific' showed no superiority over the Gresley 'Pacific' and was inferior in accessibility of mechanism, the latter engine was naturally adopted as a standard class by the LNER. Twelve had been built before October 1923 and forty more during 1924. The fifth North Eastern 'Pacific' was not running till March 1924, but it was clear that unless the last three of these engines were markedly superior to their two predecessors, they were unlikely to be given the most important classes of work on the LNER. They were, in fact, all withdrawn from service by the end of 1937.

Some North Eastern enginemen got reasonably good work out of the Raven 'Pacifics' by studying their weaknesses and handling them accordingly but few men would take any special trouble in this way, especially after they had found what the Gresley 'Pacifics' could do.

Perhaps the brightest published effort by a Raven 'Pacific' was that of No 2402 in taking 245 tons from Darlington to York in a net time of rather less than 41 minutes, sustaining 79 mph on the level for some miles. This was, however, within the capacity of a Class Z 'Atlantic'. 'Pacific' No 2404 once made the same journey of 44.1 miles in 47 minutes net with a load of 445 tons. This was recorded in the *Railway Magazine* for April 1925 and referred to a period when Gresley 'Pacifics' were not doing much better on that part of the LNER.

A tendency to heated bearings in Raven 'Pacifics' naturally restrained enginemen from working them really hard as also did their heavy coal consumption. This was never reduced, as was that of Gresley 'Pacifics' by rational re-design of valves and valve-gear. Enginemen themselves could overcome some minor defects. For example, judicious application of strong string to the pipe that led steam to the reversing-gear could obviate vibration that would otherwise eventually break the pipe.

There were enginemen who did all they could to get the best out of the Raven 'Pacifics', but there were others who, resentful of innovation, did not, and there were still others who were just frightened by the sheer size of the biggest North Eastern engines. To some people the Raven 'Pacifics' looked longer than any engine ought to be and to some firemen the size of the 41 sq ft fire-grate was an outrage. No engine, they said, needed a grate as big as that, and so no-one should be expected to take any care in trying to fire it properly.

So press reports of the running of Class 4-6-2 were a record of uneven and generally uninspiring performance. This must have been depressing to those many people who saw grace besides power in the long, fat boiler-barrel, but others were so captivated by the whole aspect of the engines as to ignore the lack of evidence that it was any better than a Z.

Whether any sustained effort was made to get the very best out of Class 4–6–2 by modifying details in the light of experience is doubtful. It seems unlikely, however, that it could ever have been made appreciably superior to the Gresley 'Pacific' and so Class 4–6–2 was allowed to work itself out. There simply was no room for two entirely different designs of 'Pacific' on one railway, even one so large as the LNER.

CHAPTER 5

SOME TEST RESULTS

S OON after construction in 1889 the first two Class J 'singles'
made some test-runs and certain of the test-figures were
published.

The first Class J 4-2-2, No 1517, on test ran from Newcastle
to Berwick at a start-to-stop average of 51.5 mph with a load of
270 tons. On another run with about 150 tons, the engine is said
to have attained 90 mph in some unspecified vicinity. Over
fifty years had to elapse before there was any reliable report of a
'ninety' on this route.

In *The Engineer* for March 7, 1890 appeared some figures
derived from the measured performance of No 1518 while
working special trains between Newcastle and Berwick and re-
productions of certain indicator diagrams. A particular excerpt
from this record has often been quoted but it is hard to imagine
that anyone ever really believed it. This was the development of
1069 Indicated Horse Power (i.e. power exerted on the pistons)
while the engine was handling a train of 224 tons on the level at
86 (eighty-six) miles per hour.

Someone once somewhere carelessly attributed this snippet to
Mr. Charles Rous-Marten but in the *Railway Magazine* for April
1906 he sternly disowned it, adding that any reference he may
have made to these figures was only for the purpose of declaring
his disbelief in their accuracy. And well he might! In 1890 it was
unusual for a speed of even 80 mph to be attained by any train in
Great Britain even when running down gradients as steep as 1 in
200. It is doubtful whether 'eighty' had ever been reached on the
level. Even twenty years later it was unusual even for Great

Western 4-6-0s to get up to 86 mph even on the most favourable gradients.

In *The Engineer* for March 14, 1890 there was reproduced a letter from 'E.B.D.' who expressed extreme difficulty in believing that No 1518 had in fact reached 86 mph on the level. This generated a stream of column-length readers' letters that continued until May 9, 1890. In this controversy, fairy tales, irrelevances, smoke screens and red herrings were flaunted with a fervour barely to be surpassed by readers of the popular railway journals sixty years later. No one pointed out that on the basis of other figures in the report, the speed of 86 mph was impossible.

The total running resistance of engine, tender and train is proportional to the ratio of indicated horse power to speed on the level. The report quotes 1041 IHP at 75 mph on the level and the ratio of these is 13.9. But 1069 IHP at 86 mph gives only 12.4. So anyone who believes the quoted figures must also believe that raising the speed from 75 to 86 mph *reduced* the running resistance by over 10 per cent.

The power required to haul a train on the level varies approximately as the square of the speed. If the 1041 IHP at 75 mph be accepted, then 1069 IHP corresponds to 76 mph and this is credible whereas 86 mph is entirely inconsistent with the other figures in the report and with wide experience of locomotive performance at the time. One may suggest that a quarter-mile timing of 11.8 seconds corresponding to 76.2 mph may have led through hasty reading of a slide-rule to the purely fictitious 86 mph. The calculator properly suppressed the '2' as being insignificant but wrote '8' instead of '7'. It's easily done!

In parenthesis it may be mentioned that on the basis of published information about the running resistance of various types of contemporary passenger vehicles generally similar to those of the North Eastern, it is estimated that it would have taken about 1150 IHP to run the engine and train continuously on the level at 75 mph or about 1500 IHP at 86 mph.

All the foregoing assumes, as did the controversialists in 1890, that the quoted speeds were sustained on the level, whereas the published information contains neither confirmation nor denial of the assumption. Moreover it is not stated where the train was when the observations were made at the alleged 75 mph and the alleged 86 mph.

If it be assumed that the engine could sustain 75 mph on the level (and calculation suggests that 1150 IHP rather than 1040 IHP would be required) it might have run for a short distance at 86 mph on the level in one particular vicinity. On the north-bound journey there is a drop of about 70 ft in the stretch of about 4 miles from the end of a level length including Belford and the beginning of a level length between Smeafield and Beal. Calculation suggests that if the engine worked as hard all the way down this drop as it would have to do to maintain 75 mph on the level it might just have reached 86 mph when it ran off the down gradient on to the second level but the speed would then immediately start to drop.

To summarise, it is unlikely that the engine could have maintained even 75 mph on the level, with 224 tons, but might have attained that speed on a down-gradient and kept close to it over a $\frac{1}{4}$ mile of immediately succeeding level. The speed quoted as 86 mph was far more probably 76 mph. If, however, the engine was capable of maintaining 75 mph on the level (perhaps with the help of a strong following wind) it may just have touched 86 mph at the bottom of a few miles of down-gradient averaging 1 in 300.

But however much glory the first two Class Js did achieve on the test-runs, the class as a whole did nothing distinguished in service and the engines were re-built by Wilson Worsdell as two-cylinder 'simples' in 1894-5. The Class I engines were eventually altered in the same way.

In 1898 W. M. Smith presented at the Institution of Mechanical Engineers a paper entitled 'Results of recent practical experiments with Express Locomotives' and a neat condensate of the results by E. L. Ahrons appeared in *The Railway Magazine* for May 1917. Five classes of locomotive were tested, 901, 1463, Simplified J, MI and QI. Each locomotive took a train weighing 187 tons from Newcastle to Tweedmouth and back, $65\frac{1}{2}$ miles each way, in a scheduled time of 75 minutes, i.e. at 52.3 mph, burning an average of nearly 40 pounds of coal per mile which even by contemporary standards was very high for such a light train. Coal consumption varied from class to class between 2.9 and 3.65 lb per indicated horsepower hour and these figures were not bad for 'wet steam' engines in 1898. Unfortunately they are extremely suspect as it is difficult to credit the figures quoted for indicated horsepower. In the first instance they are given to an absurd degree of superficial precision (e.g. 645.9 for Class M1) whereas the uncertainty in taking an indicator diagram on a locomotive and afterwards measuring it amounts to hardly less than 10 per cent in each direction. But apart from that the figures are far too high by comparison with what is known from much later research to be reasonable.

A feature particularly criticized in the discussion following presentation of the paper was the use of a single indicator for two (or four?) cylinder-ends. Inevitably the pipe-connection with the cylinder must have been long and the indication thus quite unreliable. Mr. Michael Longridge doubted some of the figures for boiler efficiency on the ground that water carried over with the steam ought not to be counted as water evaporated by the boiler.

Most commentators were critical and many of those present must have been glad when Mr. Longridge pierced the gloom irreverently and perhaps irrelevantly by saying: 'Mr. Worsdell was to be congratulated upon having found an engine that would run his trains to time. If he would put such engines on the trains of the North Eastern Railway and run them to time, the public would be much indebted to him.'

A summary of the paper was presented in *The Engineer* for November 4, 1898 and a leader in the same issue commented on it in unflattering terms, including:

'Mr. Smith has placed before his hearers a great mass of figures which he leaves them to digest for themselves as they please. It is not likely that any assimilation will be pushed far. Indeed the attempt to deduce any law or to co-ordinate any facts would lead to lunacy. We encounter at every moment the most baffling contradictions. The incongruities are amazing; the incompatibles perplexing.'

Readers may wonder how information that warranted such criticizm came to be submitted to the Institution of Mechanical Engineers as the basis of a paper to be presented at a meeting, and having been submitted, how it came to be accepted. A possible explanation is that the author, having failed to make much sense of the figures, hoped that comments on the paper might contain some help for him, and that the Institution concurred in this artifice.

In 1902 W. M. Smith presented at the same Institution a paper on 'The application of cylindrical steam distributing valves to locomotives.' These were the 'segmented piston valves' associated with his name and in a six-month test in ordinary service a Class M1 engine fitted with them averaged 29.55 lb of coal per mile whilst of eleven corresponding locomotives with flat valves the lowest consumption was 32.33 lb per mile and the average 34.08. This was pretty convincing evidence that piston valves could be made worthwhile.

During the discussion doubts were raised, because of possible steam leakage, as to the maintenance of this advantage over long mileage. Segmental piston valves are 'bitty' and Sir E. H. Carbutt asked why no use seemed to be made of solid valve-heads each with three rings as everyone had done for pistons themselves over the preceding forty-odd years. Thirty years after the meeting the hint had been taken, tested and proved and multi-ring piston valves accepted as the best means of minimizing leakage over high mileages. As they afforded no possible means of relief of high cylinder-pressure produced by trapping water, they had to be accompanied by a relief valve on each cylinder-cover, and W. M. Smith had found that provision to be necessary even in conjunction with his spring-loaded segmented piston-valves.

CHAPTER 6

USE OF STEAM

—————

Compound Engines

WITH the general principle of multi-stage expansion well accepted in stationary steam engines and in marine steam engines, and with Webb actively pursuing the compound principle in North Western engines, T. W. Worsdell whilst still on the Great Eastern probably thought 'We mustn't be left behind'. He decided, very reasonably, to try the compound principle in its simplest possible form (with two cylinders only) with the primary purpose of finding out whether it did in fact show any significant saving of fuel. If it did, then the use of more than two cylinders could warrant consideration. So he built some two-cylinder compound 4-4-os with Joy valve-gear but these engines, whether economical or not, were certainly not fast and so could not be regarded as successful. Nevertheless, even after taking charge of North Eastern locomotives Worsdell still thought compounding to be worth trying. It may be useful to consider what might have led him to that belief.

As soon as steam engines began to discharge their exhaust steam into the open air, intelligent observers recognized that in doing so they were throwing away a lot of energy. The obvious question was 'Why can't we get that steam to do some more work before we let it go?' This gave rise to the obvious suggestion to pass the steam exhausted from one cylinder into another cylinder where it could do some more useful work before it got away. Such re-use of steam could be repeated until its pressure was so little higher than atmospheric pressure that what little extra work it might do was too small to justify the expense and complication of another cylinder.

In a stationary power plant there is usually room for extra cylinders and indeed also for a condenser so that steam may be discharged into a vacuum giving the advantage of up to 14 lb per sq in extra pressure. In such circumstances 2-stage, 3-stage and 4-stage expansion of steam were successfully used.

In a steam locomotive, however, space was limited and no condenser was worthwhile because discharge of exhaust steam to the atmosphere was the most economical method of producing the strong draught needed for a fire hot enough to give the engine a power-weight ratio that would make it a commercial proposition. Nevertheless 'compounding'—here meaning 'two-stage expansion'—was repeatedly tried in steam locomotives but never entirely justified itself in Great Britain. Its one possible advantage is economy in fuel and, in countries where fuel was specially expensive, compound engines continued to be used. But elsewhere the greater complication of the compound engine and its heavier maintenance cost offset its fuel economy to the extent that the overall advantage was negligible.

To minimize the complication of compounding, the compound locomotive should be limited to two cylinders, and this thought controlled the first application of compounding on the North Eastern Railway. It did, however, make an unsymmetrical locomotive because the first stage of expansion of steam increases its volume so that the second-stage (low pressure) cylinder needed to have a greater volume than the first-stage (high pressure) cylinder. Most British locomotive engineers preferred to avoid the asymmetry of the two-cylinder compound at the cost of the extra complication of using more than two cylinders.

In designing any compound locomotive special consideration had to be given to the operation of starting from rest. A two-cylinder simple engine, with cranks at right angles as usual could always start from rest in one direction or the other because if either crank were in a weak position at or near the 'dead centre' the other was in a strong position to develop a starting pull from

its piston-thrust. But a two-cylinder compound in normal operation applied boiler steam only to the high-pressure cylinder and
if its crank happened to be near a dead centre no starting pull
could be produced. The only way to get over this difficulty was
to apply steam to the low-pressure piston which was in its best
position for rotating the crank axle. So means had to be provided
for applying boiler steam directly to the low-pressure cylinder
at least when trying to get away from a standstill. But such steam
exerted on the high-pressure piston a force that opposed motion
in the desired direction. This could be the stronger influence with
the cranks in certain angular positions, and so the engine might
start in the wrong way if steam at boiler pressure were admitted
to the low-pressure cylinder.

To avoid this, the artifice used by T. W. Worsdell was the
'intercepting valve' in the pipe that normally conveyed steam
from the HP cylinder to the LP cylinder. It was a flap-valve,
normally open; in closing it moved into the pipe and to its seat
in the opposite direction to the normal flow of steam. If the steam
pressure on the LP side of the valve were higher than that on the
other side, it held the valve tightly on its intercepting seat. If,
however, the pressure difference were in the opposite direction
it would tend to open the valve.

To start a Worsdell two-cylinder compound, the driver opened
the regulator in the ordinary way and if she started, well and good.
If not, he closed the regulator and opened the cylinder-cocks to
empty the cylinders of steam. He then closed the cocks and pulled
a lever in the cab in line with the boiler hand-rail and this admitted
steam to a small cylinder attached to the smokebox. This caused
a piston to move forward and in doing so to close the intercepting valve. In that position the piston had uncovered a port
through which steam passed to the LP cylinder but was prevented
by the intercepting valve from exerting any back-pressure on
the HP piston.

In that condition the engine would start as readily as any two-
cylinder simple engine (and was just as liable to 'refuse' and to
need setting back) and as soon as she did so, the driver released
the starting lever. When the driving axle had rotated far enough

for the HP valve to allow steam to escape from the HP cylinder, the pressure on the HP side of the intercepting valve would rise, while that on the LP side was diminishing because the starting valve was too small to admit more than a trickle of steam. When the pressure-difference became great enough, it forced the intercepting valve open and the engine began to run as a compound in the ordinary way.

A two-cylinder compound engine with no outside cylinders did not need to look any different from the corresponding two-cylinder 'simple' but its voice was very different. It gave only two exhaust beats in each revolution of the driving wheels instead of the familiar four. The fewer beats were heavier because each discharged twice the weight of steam that flowed with each of the four beats of the single-expansion engine. This was opposite to the natural expectation that double expansion of steam would give it a double reduction in pressure and so it would come less noisily out of the blast pipe. This reasoning was false, firstly because in compound locomotives the total expansion of steam in two stages was not greatly different from that achieved in the single stage of the 'simple', and secondly because the pressure of steam at the blast nozzle had to be made to induce the desired draught on the fire by appropriately adjusting the diameter of the nozzle. To produce steam at any particular rate a boiler required a particular pressure of steam at the blast nozzle irrespective of what the steam did in getting there from the boiler.

So compounding did not influence ferocity of exhaust but the number of beats per revolution certainly did and two-cylinder compounds were noisier than the corresponding two-cylinder simples. The noise itself was not technically important but the lower frequency of beats meant wider pulsation in draught and so a greater tendency to lose fuel in the form of cinders lifted from the fire, drawn into the smokebox and perhaps thrown out of the chimney.

All T. W. Worsdell's compounds had Joy valve-gear generally working flat valves above the cylinders (with certain exceptions in which piston valves were used) until in the J and M classes the sizes and positions of the cylinders prohibited this layout.

There is no evidence that the North Eastern ever carried out any rigorous test that might provide quantitative evidence of the coal-saving attributable to compounding. It is known, on the other hand, that when a North Eastern compound was working hard, the overall ratio of expansion of the steam was low enough to be readily attainable in a rationally designed single-expansion locomotive. The possible advantage of compounding was therefore that associated with the fact that the temperature-range in the LP cylinder was narrower than that in the cylinder of a single-stage expansion engine doing the same work. This advantage is hard to express numerically but it is certainly no greater than the observed differences in performance of nominally identical locomotives.

The North Eastern's ultimate opinion on compounding is expressed by the facts that it built only two compound engines after 1894, and that it converted its two-cylinder compounds into 'simples', in some cases after only a few years' service. As on the North Western Railway, compound goods engines survived longer than did compound passenger engines. It should be added, however, that goods engines in general lived longer than passenger engines without necessarily having run any more miles.

The necessity, in Classes J and M, to cut large holes in the frame plates to accommodate the outside steam chests was a consequence of the large diameter (28 in) of the LP cylinder. Clearly the limit in size of this layout had been almost reached. It was natural when thinking about this to realize that the next sensible step was to divide the second-stage expansion between two equal cylinders, making three in all and offering a symmetrical layout of the cylinders. This was worth trying and so the solitary Class M two-cylinder compound No 1619 was extensively rebuilt on these lines in 1898, re-introducing to the North Eastern outside cylinders in a very eyeable design. Link motion was used to work flat valves for the outside (LP) cylinders and a piston valve for the inside (HP) cylinder. The necessity for placing four eccentrics between one of the inside crank webs and the adjacent axle-box must have caused the designer to think a

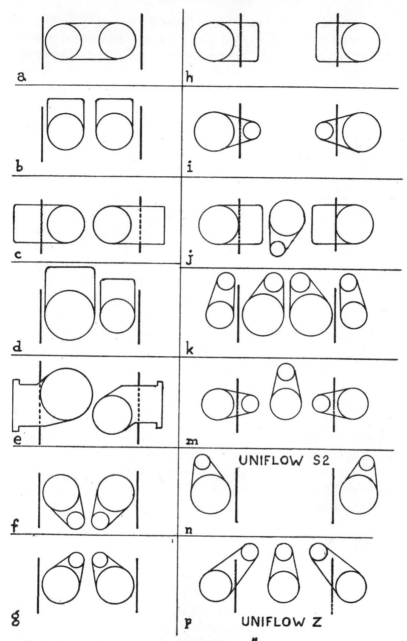

a

h

b

i

c

j

d

k

e

m

f

n UNIFLOW S2

g

p UNIFLOW Z

Fig 6 Valve and cylinder arrangements

bit and he may well have realised that this could be a prohibitive bottle-neck in a locomotive that was big enough to require thicker crank-webs and wider axle-boxes than those of No 1619.

This type of three-cylinder compound was tried by several railways, in each case with a starting valve and a reducing valve or a proportional valve. This was, however, pointless complication. All that was needed for reliable starting was an extra port and pipe which fed boiler steam to the receiver when a small regulator-opening was feeding the HP cylinder. The HP piston then had equal steam pressures on both sides of it and the engine started as an ordinary two-cylinder simple with steam at boiler pressure. Once the train was well on the move, the regulator was opened wider, whereupon the feed of boiler-steam to the receiver was stopped and the engine ran as a compound in the ordinary way.

Although this type of compound locomotive was enthusiastically taken up by the Midland Railway and by the LMS to the extent that there were ultimately 240 'Midland compounds', the North Eastern built no other engine like No 1619. But Worsdell did produce two very much larger engines, Nos 730 and 731, which were four-cylinder compound 'Atlantics' with 22 in diameter LP cylinders between the frame plates and two sets of valve-gear to work four piston-valves.

At that time no British designer worried himself very much about difficulties in getting at mechanism and so the possibility of using outside valve gear on these engines is unlikely to have been considered. No 731 had what is described as a modified form of Walschaerts gear. If it was the Stévart cross-connected gear, that was a reason for keeping the mechanism between the frame plates. But Walschaerts gear in its common form would have been far better mounted in its usual place outside the frame plates.

The compounds when new showed some superiority over contemporary Class V two-cylinder simple Atlantics on the North Eastern but they never matched the best performances of the Class Z three-cylinder single Atlantics introduced in 1911.

In LNE hands, No 1619 lasted till 1930, and was thus the

longest-lived North Eastern compound, having run with two cylinders for five years and with three cylinders for thirty-two years. The four-cylinder engines Nos 730 and 731 lasted till 1935 and 1933 respectively.

Superheating
The North Eastern was a little late in beginning its experiments with superheating and had not decided whether it was worthwhile before ordering the first members of its best main line passenger train engines—the Class Z 'Atlantics'—from the North British Locomotive Company in 1911. So half of these were built as 'wet steam' engines and the others with superheaters. The latter group had mechanical lubricators as became general British practice on engines using superheated steam, and they also had pyrometers to show how hot the steam became, but these were removed as soon as it became clear that the information they gave, even when correct, was superfluous.

Superheating was tried on existing engines that had piston valves and in most cases the smokebox extension required to accommodate the superheater gave the engine a more impressive appearance.

Although the primary advantage of superheating lay in economy of coal, superheated steam is just a shade quicker in its movements than is 'saturated' steam and therefore tended to make the engine a bit faster.

No superheater gave any perceptible advantage until the engine had been working long enough and hard enough to get its fire up to full temperature and this might take five to ten minutes from a 'cold' start. Main line locomotives could reap a benefit from superheating for most of their running-time but engines engaged in shunting or in pick-up goods work might not do so. Superheaters were removed from a good many engines largely engaged on start-and-stop work.

In Table 3 some figures are given for heating surface of superheaters as originally fitted to North Eastern locomotives. But in them (as in other railways' locomotives) there were many subsequent alterations to superheaters.

Uniflow engines

In each cylinder of a steam engine, steam does useful work by pushing the piston along. In the first part of the stroke of the piston steam from the boiler 'follows up' the motion of the piston, and after connection with the boiler has been 'cut off' by the valve, the steam continues to push, although with decreasing force, because it is expanding. While that happens the steam is cooling and so when it is permitted by movement of the valve to escape to the atmosphere it returns to the valve and on the way it cools the iron walls of the passage and the edges of the ports.

The charge of boiler-steam that comes along to push the piston on its next stroke warms the walls up again by passing into them heat that will be taken away up the chimney by the next out-flow of exhaust steam. The walls of a passage used both to admit steam to a cylinder and to allow it to escape afterwards therefore provide an 'escape-route' for heat.

This disadvantage could be avoided in an engine made so that, after doing its work on the piston, steam escaped from the cylinder without re-tracing its inward path. Such an engine works on the 'uniflow' principle. (Jacob Perkins built a compound engine with 'uniflow' cylinders in 1827, two years before Stephenson's 'Rocket'.)

In the 'uniflow' engine the length of the piston is almost equal to its stroke and a ring of ports extending round the circumference of the cylinder provide means by which steam in either end-compartment of the cylinder may escape to the chimney as soon as the piston uncovers them. Steam is admitted to each end of the cylinder by a valve in the ordinary way and never returns. No item in the engine is alternately heated and cooled and so the 'uniflow' can have a higher thermal efficiency than that of the conventional steam engine.

The 'uniflow' principle was used (1849-52) in a South Eastern Railway 2-2-2 locomotive but was not sufficiently advantageous to be retained. The principle began to be successfully used in stationary steam engines near the end of the nineteenth century. It had a considerable vogue in that class of service and it reduced coal consumption by 5 to 10 per cent. It was revived for locomotives by Professor Stumpf in Germany about sixty years after its abandonment by the SER and it was applied, with his guidance, to two North Eastern locomotives, a modified class S2 4-6-0 No 825 in 1913 and a modified Class Z 'Atlantic' No 2212 in 1919.

In the first case the appearance of the engine (built as a 'uniflow' immediately after the last Class S2 in 1913) must have startled most onlookers because of the large highly-placed cylinders, the unwonted exposure of driving wheels and the use of Walschaerts valve gear. This worked large piston-valves through 'step-up' rocking levers that caused the valve to move about 50 per cent further than did the end of the radius rod.

In normal running each piston-valve admitted steam to the two cylinder-ends in turn but did not deal with exhaust steam because that escaped through the central belt of exhaust ports. But when the valves had maximum travel or something near it, they permitted steam to escape to exhaust in the usual way through the admission ports before the piston had opened the central belt of ports to exhaust. Some provision of this kind was necessary in a 'uniflow' locomotive in order that it should not be inferior to a conventional locomotive in getting away from a standing start. When the engine was worked at any usual 'cut-off' for normal running, the valve travel was too short to open the ports to exhaust.

Because fast running left very little time for the steam in a cylinder to escape when the central exhaust ports were uncovered by the piston, those ports were made with a large cross-sectional area, with the result that the exhaust was so rapid as to sound explosive. It is said that No 825 was so arrestingly distinctive in this respect that her use on trains on the North Eastern main line between York and Darlington made a noticeable difference to egg-production rates on poultry farms close to the main line. Unsatisfactory as is this report in that it fails to say whether the farmers got more eggs or fewer it shows that locomotive design can have unexpected effects in other fields of endeavour.

In *The Railway Magazine* for July 1913, Mr. C. J. Allen reported a run in a 265 ton train behind No 825 from Darlington to York. He thought the run was dismal even though 'Old Stumpy' came through Thirsk at 66 mph and gained 2 minutes on the scheduled time of 51 minutes. No 825 was rebuilt as a standard Class S2 in 1924.

In comparative tests on express passenger trains averaging 330 tons at 51 mph No 825 burned from 4 to $4\frac{1}{2}$ lb of coal per drawbar horse power hour. This was not brilliant for an engine using superheated steam, but the competing Class S2 locomotive No 797 needed over 10 per cent more. On goods trains of about 800 tons running at about 24 mph the engines came out equal at a creditable 3.3 lb per DHP hour. On estimated coal consumption per Indicated Horse Power hour, the uniflow averaged 2.6 lb against 2.8 lb for No 797. Such a small difference could not justify adoption of the 'uniflow' principle.

The last Class Z Atlantic No 2211 was built in 1918 and shortly afterwards Darlington turned out No 2212, a 'uniflow' version of Class Z. The cylinders were at normal height but their length demanded an extension of the wheel-base of the bogie; apart from this, the difference in external appearance between No 2212 and the standard Class Z was remarkably small.

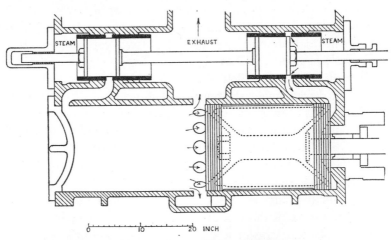

Fig 7 Uniflow cylinder and valve

The three valves were placed with their centre-lines in a plane some $17\frac{1}{2}$ in above that of the cylinder centre-lines and the two

outer valves were 34 in apart. The distance between the centre-
line of each outside cylinder and that of its valve was 26 in, so
that the clearance volume was very large and high expansion
ratio impracticable. The clearance volume of the inside cylinder
was normal. Each valve was driven by Stephenson gear through
a lever that multiplied the motion by about $1\frac{1}{2}$.

In both these 'uniflow' engines the piston valves were $7\frac{1}{2}$ inches
in diameter with lap of 1.6 inches. In conjunction with the $16\frac{1}{2}$
in cylinders these dimensions would normally make for a very
fast engine but there is no evidence that No 2212 ever distinguished herself for speed. The large clearance volume of the
outside cylinders probably nullified the advantage of large port
openings in admitting steam to the cylinders.

That the general running characteristics of No 2212 were not
bad may be judged from the fact that she survived as a 'uniflow'
till 1935, when she was withdrawn from service and eventually
rebuilt with new cylinders and Lentz poppet valves. In January
1920 Mr. C. J. Allen reported that No 2212 with a load of 560
tons took over 47 minutes to cover the thirty miles from a start
at York to a stop at Northallerton. This was a black mark for
'uniflow' as on at least two occasions, comparably loaded
standard Class Z engines had made the same journey in 36 minutes.

It would seem that no fuel economy achieved by the 'uniflow'
system was great enough to justify the extra cost and maintenance
charges of these non-standard North Eastern engines.

The uniflow system eliminated a loss occasioned by a tem-
perature-difference associated with expansion ratio. So the big
advantage from the Uniflow system might have been expected
only where the expansion ratio was high. It might therefore have
been sensible to fit No 825 and No 2212 with cylinders having a
markedly higher swept volume than the standard ones so that
the work could have been done at higher expansion ratios than
was usual in Class S2. But cylinders much larger than those
actually used might have been prohibited by limitations of space
and weight.

Any experimental innovation that did not justify further
application might be classed as

1. Good enough to be retained for a normal life of about thirty years; or
2. Good enough to be retained till the next major overhaul; or
3. Bad enough to justify immediate abandonment.

The North Eastern three-cylinder compound and the four-cylinder compounds came into Class 1. Uniflow No 825 and 'uniflow' No 2212 came somewhere between Classes 1 and 2.

Cab-fittings

The drawing on page 136 shows the cab-fittings in Class M1 4-4-0 No 1621 substantially as preserved in York Museum, and this may be taken as representative of the cab layout in the smaller Wilson Worsdell designs.

North Eastern coaches had air-brakes, for which the control handle (Item 21) in the cab was well placed for a driver looking through his front window, but rather a long way (30 in) from the cab side-openings through which the driver had to lean when backing the engine up to a vehicle for coupling.

The vacuum brake handle was very awkward to reach from any point in the cab. One reason for this may be that as the general layout of cabs of North Eastern engines had been decided before there was any thought of a need to control vacuum brakes, the equipment for that purpose had to be fitted into what space was left, whether the driver would find it convenient or not.

In normal running the enginemen stood on wooden 'pedestals' about a foot high; firing had to be done from a stance in the space less than two feet wide, between the pedestals. This seems very awkward, as a natural stance for firing would require the gap to be widened by about a foot on the left hand side. But of course one can get used to anything and this layout did at least permit the fireman to get some support from the pedestal for his left leg and from the inside of the wheel-splasher for his bottom. So he could be well braced for right hand curves in the track, but less happy on left hand bends.

On top of the left hand wheel-splasher there was space for a 6 ft man to lie flat and indeed there was almost room for two.

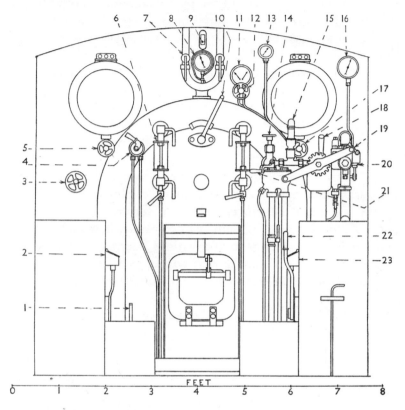

Fig 8 Interior of cab of Class M1

1. Damper handle
2. Oil-box for rear axle-box
3. Blower handwheel
4. Steam-sanding valve
5. Handwheel for steam to LH injector
6. Boiler-water gauge
7. Whistle valve
8. Boiler pressure gauge
9. Tail of safety-valve lever
10. Regulator handle
11. Duplex gauge for air-brake
12. Handwheel for steam to ejector
13. Carriage-heating steam pressure-gauge
14. Stop-valve for steam to air-pump
15. Air-pressure regulator
16. Vacuum gauge
17. Handwheel for steam to RH injector
18. Vacuum brake handle
19. Reversing handle
20. Vacuum brake ejector
21. Air-brake handle
22. Cylinder-cock lever
23. Oil-box for rear axle-box

So although the cab was not ideal for the enginemen to work in, it could offer unusual repose in waiting periods.

There is no exceptional fitting in the cab but it may be mentioned that Item 15 is the standard Westinghouse air-operated steam valve that starts the air pump as soon as the air pressure in the reservoir falls below 90 lb per sq in.

The fire-hole was exposed by lifting the tab above the tray to release the main fire door which could then be swung downwards and outwards about the horizontal hinge-pin at its bottom edge.

The fire was normally fed, however, through the small rectangular opening in the main door, after the 'trap-door' had been opened by using the shovel to push it forward with rotation about the horizontal hinge-pin at its top edge. It would remain in any one of a number of angular settings determined by engagement of a projection from it with ratchet teeth in a curved bar projecting backwards from a pivot-pin above the trap-door.

CHAPTER 7

SOME MECHANICAL DETAILS

Exhaust-cock

ALTHOUGH in writing about the 'exhaust-cock' dispute it has been customary to refer to exhaust-cocks in the plural, this must not be taken to imply that there was more than one cock per engine. It is impossible to be dogmatic about what was or was not done in details of locomotive construction in the Fletcher period but it can be said of Fletcher 2–4–0 No 910 in York Museum that it has a single exhaust-cock, and of Tennant No 1463 that it has two. The single cock on No 910 is shown in Fig 9. It is in a short

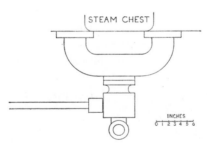

Fig 9   Exhaust-cock on Fletcher 2–4–0

vertical pipe attached to the underside of a U-shaped pipe that connected the two exhaust spaces. When the cock was opened it allowed part of the exhaust steam to escape through a $1\frac{3}{4}$ in pipe pointing forward. The cock was worked by a lever on the driver's side of the cab.

Tennant No 1463 has a similar cock, and in addition a second one connected to a pipe extending backwards to end under the ashpan. These cocks are worked by separate handles on the fireman's side of the cab.

It almost looks as if Tennant desired to placate the Geordies on this particular subject and, to use a phrase unknown at that time, to 'fall over backwards' in doing so. He gave them not only one cock, but two, and placed the handles conveniently for the fireman who was, after all, the man most concerned by bad steaming of the engine.

The purpose of cocks with opposite-facing discharge pipes on an engine that normally ran chimney first is not easy to imagine. One can see that the backward discharge pipe would keep the escaping steam away from the mechanism of the engine when running forward, but was there much to be gained by being similarly fussy about the short periods for which the engine was running backwards? Or, if so, could not the cock be closed during those periods?

Or, taking up another thought, is the present backward leading pipe only part of a connection by which water in the tender-tank could be heated by exhaust steam or part of a connection to an exhaust steam injector?

There is thus doubt about the exact details of what was done by Fletcher or by Tennant but it may be useful to comment on the essential principles governing the possible utility of allowing exhaust steam to leak from its normal passage to the blast pipe.

As the exhaust steam in any conventional locomotive was made to do the vital job of keeping the fire going by shooting from the blast-pipe to the chimney and inducing flue-gases to go with it, what was the object of letting some of the steam get away without helping in that essential work? The answer is that by varying the extent of what amounted to a leakage of steam from the bottom of the blast-pipe, the draught inducing power of the blast-pipe could be varied without altering the position or size of anything in the smokebox. In a gale of sulphurous gas and cinders, mechanism does not long remain in good order and so variable blast-pipes always tended to be troublesome. The Fletcher exhaust-cock produced the effects of a variable blast-pipe although it was itself well away from the smokebox. This seems so highly satisfactory that one suspects at once that it must have been disadvantageous in some way and so it was.

The draught-inducing power of a steam-jet depends on the weight of steam discharged per second and on the speed of the steam, which is determined by its pressure at the blast-nozzle. If part of the steam is allowed to escape through an exhaust-cock, the flow per second through the nozzle is reduced. If the draught is to be retained at its original intensity, the speed of the steam must be increased, and therefore the pressure behind it must be increased (by reducing the diameter of the blast-nozzle) and with it the back pressure on the pistons. So an exhaust system that is to produce enough draught with an exhaust-cock open, must develop in that condition a higher back-pressure than would suffice if the exhaust-cock were closed. The engine suffers a permanent disadvantage in normal running so that its blast may be variable without having mechanism in the smokebox.

It is interesting to note that, over sixty years after No 901 was built, the LNER tried the exhaust-cock principle in a big 2–8–2 but they placed the cock (a butterfly valve) in the smokebox. There the valve was troublesome and so it was replaced by a plug-valve which was worse. The next attempt was to have been made with a flap-valve but World War II was at that time running into one of its worst phases and the project was dropped.

Reversing gear

On the vast majority of British locomotives hand-power was used for setting the valve mechanism for forward running or backward running and for the desired cut-off. On a small engine the effort required to alter the setting of the valve-gear was small enough to permit the use of a reversing lever. On larger engines, screw-type reversing was the natural means of bringing the necessary hand-effort within the reasonable range of an average driver. Reversing was infrequent on any engine doing a main-line job and so a stiff reversing gear, although a nuisance, was not a fatal defect. At the other extreme, on a shunting engine, the reversing gear had to work easily and quickly. Lever reverse was ideal on a small shunting engine, but for a larger one, power reverse was the next step.

North Eastern 'Atlantics' and most of the later classes had 'steam reversing gear'. This means that the reversing shaft was rotated by applying steam from the boiler to one end or the other of a cylinder containing a piston on the same rod as a similar piston in another cylinder (the 'cataract' cylinder) of which the two ends were connected by a pipe and kept full of water. The common piston rod was extended and linked to an arm on the reversing shaft.

By closing a valve in the pipe and thus prohibiting passage of water between the two ends of the cataract cylinder, the piston was prevented from moving and the reversing gear thus locked.

On a shunting engine that did not need to hold any position of the reversing gear for more than a minute or two at a stretch, this was satisfactory. In other classes of service, however, leakage past the piston made the 'lock' ineffective and, in running, the 'cut-off' would gradually become later than the driver's original selection and if he did not intervene the engine would set itself in full gear.

North Eastern designers evidently feared worse defects than this, as their steam reversing gear was fitted as an adjunct to lever reversing gear so that hand power could be used if steam should fail. In the later versions the lever in the cab stood no higher than the quadrant, but a long lever was provided for fitting into the 'stub' if and when the power gear failed.

Piston valves

Piston valves were tried, with justifiable caution, by the North Eastern in the 1890s and the 'segmental' type associated with the name of W. M. Smith was eventually adopted. But there were evidently doubts and differences of opinion as to whether they were worthwhile.

For example, in 1894 the simple rebuilt form of Class J included 8 in piston valves above the cylinders. But flat valves were used in Class Q and in the two intended 'flyers' of Class Q1. Three years later came Class R with $8\frac{3}{4}$ in piston valves below the

cylinders and Class S with flat valves. The generally similar Class
S1 two years later had piston valves, but of the contemporary
0-8-0s about half had piston valves and the others had flat valves.
After that, piston valves became the rule, but in Class R1 they
were placed above the cylinders.

It is difficult to see any advantage in placing the valves below
the cylinders in a 4-4-0. In a 0-6-0, however, valves below the
cylinders might also be below the leading axle and the extreme
height of the cylinder/valve block was then less than with valves
above the cylinders and so the boiler could have a lower pitch.
This was no doubt something to be borne in mind when Gateshead was thinking of putting a 5 ft 6 in boiler on a 0-6-0.

As was common at the time, the North Eastern failed to
separate piston valve heads so widely as to minimize the length
of the passages from the valve to the cylinder. Piston valves
applied to outside cylinders of North Eastern engines were themselves well inside the frame and the steam passages were much
longer than those (for example) in Great Western 4-6-0s.

Tail-rods

Tail-rods were provided for the 19 in pistons in the rebuilds of
Class J, in Class R 4-4-0s and in some other North Eastern
engines. They were also used by some other British railways in
the decade before World War I but eventually they were all
abandoned.

The idea behind the tail-rod was that it would convey some of
the weight of the piston to the tail-rod bush but it does not seem
that that was so well able to carry weight as was the cylinder
itself. There were probably differences of opinion at Gateshead
about this and the question as to whether it was worthwhile to
provide tubular shrouds for the tail-rods. This was done on Class
T2 of 1913, and to varying extents on some other North Eastern
engines.

The pretty two-cylinder compound 2-2-4T *Aerolite* in York
Museum has the odd feature of a tail-rod for the low-pressure
piston but not for the other.

Anti-vacuum valve

An interesting detail applied to the Class J as 'simplified' and to many subsequent Worsdell engines was an anti-vacuum device that 'spoiled' the vacuum not by air but by steam. So when the regulator was closed and the moving pistons reduced steam-chest pressure below a predetermined figure a valve responded and fed steam to the steam-chests. The main advantage was not that the engine 'drifted' more easily, but that the tendency for smoke-box gases to be drawn into the cylinder was markedly reduced and with it the tendency to carbonize the oil on the pistons and piston-valves.

In every engine the build-up of carbonaceous matter on ports always occurred to a greater or lesser extent and was trouble-some in several ways. It could be avoided by never allowing the engine to run with the regulator quite closed, but British drivers in general would not take the trouble to maintain this condition.

The 'automatic' steam valve was a good move in a very useful direction, but it was another gadget on the engine and could be a nuisance, for example, by allowing steam to leak into the steam-chests when the engine was standing and thus creating a risk of unexpected movement, unless the driver had remembered to open the cylinder-cocks.

Petticoat pipes

In common with some other British railways during the period 1900–15, the North Eastern encumbered smokeboxes with 'petticoat pipes' (Fig 3 page 68) in the hope of making the blast more efficient by inducing more draught with no more back pressure. None of these survived for many years and none of them need have been tried. The very practical researches of Professor Goss at Purdue University in 1904 established that no combination of petticoat pipes was any better than a plain blast-pipe and chimney ideally proportioned for the normal running conditions of the engine.

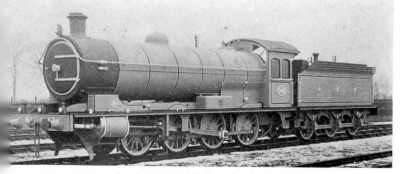

4. No 825 (Class S2 with Stumpf uniflow cylinders). Walschaerts valve-gear with multiplying lever. Pyrometer lead from superheater

5. No 846 (Class S3). Cylinder well below raised running-board

6. No 2116 (Class T1). Long front overhang associated with length of piston tail-rod

7. No 1247 (Class T2). Pop safety-valves. Fireman's part of regulator handle visible through front window

38. No 901 (Class T3). Three-cylinder engine. Frame extended forward to keep buffer-beam clear of piston tail-rods

39. No 1667 (Class U). Smaller-wheeled version of Class N

40. No 649 (Class V). Crosshead almost hidden. Double Ramsbottom safety-valves in large brass casing

41. No 696 (Class VI). Class V modified, for example in coupled wheel-splashers and running-board

Cab-signalling

The term 'cab-signalling' is used here as a name for any system that causes something on an engine to give to the driver information about a fixed signal that he is about to pass. Many railways tentatively tried such devices for short or long periods but until after World War II only the Great Western system was used extensively or for many years in Great Britain.

On the North Eastern, a system credited to V. L. Raven and C. Baister, was first tried in November 1895 and in two or three years was in regular use at some 120 signals on the main line. Close to each such signal the upper end of an arm projecting vertically upwards from a spindle rotated about an axis parallel to the sleepers was in the path of the lower end of an arm projecting downwards from a similar spindle on the locomotive. The hanging arm was rotated by contact between the arms and its motion admitted air to a whistle in the cab. The sound told the driver that he was passing a signal in the 'on' position; he acknowledged the warning and cancelled it by re-setting the apparatus so that the whistle ceased to sound.

The action of pulling the signal 'off' moved the track arm out of its normal position and engines could pass without sounding the whistle. This was admirable in giving the driver a positive indication that the fixed signal, if a 'distant', was warning him to reduce speed or, if other than a 'distant', was telling him to stop right there.

But the system violated a basic principle in signalling by implying that so long as he heard nothing, the driver was all right in keeping going. Nevertheless it was highly regarded by most enginemen (it would have been very remarkable if no one had raised any objection) and it is not recorded as having led anyone into trouble. It was in use between Newcastle and Alnmouth before the end of 1899 and eventually covered the main line from Shaftholme Junction (near Doncaster) to Berwick.

Most engineers must have been uneasy about the basic mechanical principle of this system, because impact can generate very great forces with the constant danger of breaking something. In the North Eastern system this danger was minimized, not by making moving components very strong and heavy, but by the opposite artifice of making them flexible and light. Of trial outfits set up at twenty high-speed locations on North Eastern main lines, one at Croxdale showed no serious deterioration of the crucial components even after some 47,000 impacts.

Signal engineers in general were reluctant to use signal wires for any purpose additional to the primary one of moving the signal arm, but the North Eastern installations do not seem to have suffered from their departure in this respect from accredited practice.

The vast majority of enginemen who have ever lived ran nearly all their mileage without any form of cab-signalling. The North Eastern used a simple system that helped engine-drivers greatly by virtually eliminating the risk of unknowingly running past a signal 'on'. But the next thing that Raven did in this field was to introduce a much more complicated system using electricity (electricity seems to have had a fascination for mechanical engineers at about that time) that gave (when it worked properly) more information about the aspects of signals but with no extra advantage in safety. This system was much less extensively applied than was the original one; neither of them long survived the grouping of railways in 1923.

CHAPTER 8

POWER ON THE ROAD

A FTER one has been impressed by the work of this or that
class of locomotive or this or that railway in hauling trains
from here to there it is natural to seek some yardstick of comparison between the various classes.

Mere speed is in itself no figure of merit as it is obviously
affected by load and gradient. Power output takes these into
account, but potential power depends on the size of the locomotive and so one seeks an assessment of quality in a figure
relating power to size. Potential power is limited by various
elements in a locomotive. Grate area is one of these; it is basic
because it is on the grate that energy is released and it is basic in
that it is a dimension that cannot be appreciably increased without
re-boilering the locomotive and perhaps re-building it. In the
following, drawbar horsepower per sq ft of grate is calculated
for each of a number of distinctive runs by various classes of
North Eastern locomotive on a particular stretch of line.

The York–Darlington part of the North Eastern main-line is
not representative of all its main lines, but it is a well-known
'racing stretch' on which all the North Eastern main line engines
have exerted themselves at one time or another. If in examining
performance of the various locomotive-classes one confines one-
self for simplicity to a single stretch of line, this is undoubtedly
the best stretch for the purpose.

The figures quoted in Table 1 are based on published records
of runs in each direction between York and Darlington, and in
particular on the average speeds of the trains between Poppleton

Junction and Eryholme, a distance of 37.3 miles with an average adverse gradient of 1 in 1920.

By the Johansen formula the horsepower required per ton of train running over this length can be estimated by multiplying the average speed by the same number plus six for a northbound journey or minus six for a southbound journey and then dividing by 1900. By multiplying the result by the ratio of the weight of the train in tons to the grate-area of the locomotive in sq ft one obtains a numerical assessment of the drawbar horsepower per unit of grate area and this is a measure of the power of the locomotive in relation to its size.

In spite of the apparent precision of some of the figures in the table, one must beware of drawing any hair-splitting conclusions from them. The resistance of a train on a nearly level track is quite seriously dependent on the strength and direction of the wind. No information about this is available in respect of any of the trips examined here.

On the basis used in Table 1, Classes R and Z1 were outstanding, the former more remarkably so as the engine was not at the time provided with a superheater. At a perceptibly lower level came Classes Q, R1, V and 4CC. After that Classes S2, S1 and V1 formed a closely following 'tail'.

The figure 37 represents a high-class standard for a running time of 35 to 40 minutes by comparison with the average of hundreds of records of efforts by a wide range of British locomotives fitted with superheaters. As the Class R engine (No 2013) was using saturated steam in achieving these performances it may be said to have been beating the high-class standard by a few per cent.

Run No 1, timed by Mr. C. J. Allen in 1912, was notable for the unusually heavy load. Near the end of World War I considerably bigger trains even than this were sometimes taken by Class Z engines but in no recorded case did the power output reach that of No 732 on this occasion. The top speed on the level was 61.6 mph corresponding to about 1100 drawbar horsepower.

Run No 5, also timed by Mr. Allen, was notable because near the end the engine was 'opened out' a bit more and reached 71.4

mph on the level beyond Beningbrough. This corresponds to about 1000 drawbar horsepower.

On run No 7, again timed by Mr. Allen, the train touched 74 mph on the level before Beningbrough. This also means about 1000 drawbar horsepower or about 42 per sq ft of grate area for a minute or two.

The Darlington–York part of the North Eastern main line attracted attention because the train booked to make the journey in 43 minutes was for a time the 'fastest train in the British Empire'. But only one train a day had that timing; others were allowed 47 minutes or more, and with the usual load, the usual class of engine was not taxed by the usual timing.

North of Newcastle the usual schedules were about as easy as the average south of Darlington. The fastest train was (in most periods) the continuation northward of the 9.38 am from Leeds. The 10.00 am from King's Cross (the 'Flying Scotsman' of later years) was a heavier train and it was allowed about 150 minutes (there were variations of a minute or two from year to year) for the 124.4 miles from Newcastle Central to Edinburgh (Waverley). This sloth was permitted because of the agreement between the West Coast (North Western and Caledonian) group and the East Coast (Great Northern, North Eastern and North British) group on the subject of publicly booked times between London and Scotland. But the generosity of the Newcastle–Edinburgh timing could be used as a 'recovery margin' by the right type of men, who might beat the booking very handsomely if they had been late in leaving Newcastle and had their own reason for wanting to 'clock out' on time.

On one such occasion, Class Z No 722 left Newcastle with the 'Scotsman', weighing 400 tons all told, some 25 minutes late as the result of an exceptional delay further south and made the times recorded in Table 2.

It needed some vigour to get that train through Cramlington (9.9 miles) in 14 min 45 sec and by keeping going at the same pitch all the way, the Z got the 'Scotsman' into 'the Waverley' in less than 133 minutes from Newcastle. She was through Berwick in $1\frac{1}{2}$ minutes less than 'even time' from Cramlington and passed Portobello inside 'even time' from Grantshouse. Down Cockburnspath the top speed was 72 mph, not quite so high as the 74 mph noted earlier at Chathill, and so there could be no criticizm that any time had been gained by 'letting go' on the steepest downhill. There is a common tendency to suspect this on such occasions, and indeed there is a risk that a driver will unconsciously 'scamp' speed-restrictions when in a hurry, but in this case the times show that the engine worked hard all the way, and do not imply risky running anywhere.

The unusal energy was entirely consistent with a particular desire of the fireman to get to Edinburgh as fast as he could. A promise to take his wife to the cinema could explain how this Z came to show what she could do. Alternatively the driver may have been cozened by a silver handshake with an anxious passenger at Newcastle to believe that he would be more substantially rewarded at Edinburgh if he had picked up some time on the way. This kind of thing was certainly done on occasion. Some passengers even thought that 'tipping' the guard of the train might help and there is a legend that one guard responded by promising to 'tell the driver no' to be humbugged wi' the signals'.

Reference to such flippancy may seem out of place in a discourse on steam engines, but it is included here to emphasize that an unusually bright performance did not necessarily imply unusual virtue in the engine, the coal or the crew, it might simply mean that the enginemen were hurrying for some purpose of their own and could do the same again whenever they chose.

There was a touch of sadness about the fastest recorded running of Class Z engines between Darlington and York, as it was made as a farewell salute by a driver during his last week in charge of express trains before transference to less exacting duties in compliance with a rule about age. (No. 2163 p. 111).

CHAPTER 9

RUNNING COST

THE first responsibility of a locomotive engine is that it shall
run its trains to time. Whether it discharges that responsibility
on any particular occasion may be checked by any passenger with
a watch. Time-keeping is thus an easily verifiable aspect of performance. No other feature of performance in ordinary service
can be assessed with comparable precision by anyone at all.

Coal consumption per unit of useful work done in pulling a
train might be ascertained with an uncertainty of a few per cent
in each direction by trained staff using a fully equipped dynamometer car, and there is no less elaborate alternative.

In ordinary service the coal consumption of any engine per mile
run could usually be ascertained with an uncertainty of about 5
per cent each way, but no reliable estimate of the amount of work
done by the engine during any working day could be derived
from normally available information.

Nevertheless 'pounds of coal per mile' was a commonly
calculated figure. E. L. Ahrons quotes (*British Steam Locomotive*
page 234) for Class 901 engines running between Newcastle and
Edinburgh figures ranging from 1.56 to 2.64 (a variation of 50
per cent) lb of coal per coach per mile. Assuming a coach to
weigh 15 tons and the train to average 50 mph the most economical running recorded for two engines in the link was achieved
on about 4 lb per drawbar horsepower hour, which was good
for 'wet steam' engines, but those at the other end of the range
were not good.

On test runs in 1924 a Class Z 'Atlantic' consumed 3.73 lb of coal per drawbar horsepower hour and this seems to be the lowest such figure ever published in respect of any North Eastern locomotive when averaging more than 50 mph.

But cost of coal is usually less than half the running cost of a locomotive. The true cost includes that of maintenance, that associated with unavailability of the locomotive whilst it is under repair, and that of a variety of operations under the heading of 'administration'.

In the *Railway Magazine* for February 1908 some running-cost figures were given in respect of locomotives of the North Western, Great Western, Great Northern, Midland and North Eastern Railways during the year 1906. The cost per train mile ranged from 10.6 pence on the Great Northern to the maximum of 14.2 pence on the North Eastern. But here it must be remarked that the work done by a locomotive on an average train-mile was not necessarily the same on all railways.

The ratio of locomotive costs to total expenses was lowest (0.268) on the North Western and highest (0.296) on the Great Western with the North Eastern second at 0.290.

ENGINEMEN AT WORK

WATER

OLD Bob and I (said the fireman) were working the 12.20 from
Newcastle to York with the usual R and the usual train and
everything was all right till we got past Durham and then the
first thing happened. Left hand injector went off. So I tried to
start it again. After a lot of fiddling it picked up but then went
off again before I could turn round. So I started the other one—
I was glad I could!—and had another go at the left hand one but
didn't seem to get anywhere.

I put plenty on the fire and tried again. Now and again the
steam got hold of the water but soon let go. After a few more
tries I could see I was getting nowhere. Old Bob had kept an
eye on what I was doing and looked a bit puzzled when nothing
seemed to do any good. So, picking his time, he tried some tricks
himself but in the finish he had done no better than I had. So he
decided that we could do nothing and as we couldn't risk running
with only one injector he said we'd have to have another engine
from Darlington. At any rate we'd try to get one and so he
whistled a few 'crows' as we passed Ferryhill and hoped that they
would get the Darlington pilot wakened up before we got there.

As we didn't want the bother of changing engines unless we
had to, I was for going on trying to get the injector going again
but Bob said not to bother, as if it did start before we got to
Darlington we couldn't really trust it until it had been properly
examined.

Well, if you would believe it they'd managed to get another

R down to the far end of the station at Darlington ready to back on and we thought at first that we were going to have it as a pilot from there to York. But no!—that would have been too good. No!—they couldn't spare the engine and they couldn't spare the men. We had to unhook, run ahead, change on to the other R and back on with it. The stationmaster himself was there hurrying everybody along and we were ready to go only a few minutes late.

So off we struck quite happy. I had made sure that I could start both injectors and we only had to find whether the engine was a good one or not. There was nothing for us to worry about anyway, as nobody really expected you to keep time with an engine you had picked up in a hurry. There was plenty of fire in the box and so I had nothing to do for the first couple of miles except to adjust the train heater pressure and to watch how the boiler pressure and boiler water level were going. Everything was pretty normal and the engine was picking up all right. She wasn't as good as our own engine of course—you can't expect it—but she wasn't bad and in fact when the fire had burned down a bit she started to blow off. So it looked as if we were in for a smooth trip but of course you can never be sure about anything even when you're on your own engine and have got her ready and done everything yourself. But it's a good road from Darlington to York and it was a good day, clear with not much wind and as we got going past Cowton and Danby Wiske I felt that we had a good chance of picking up a bit of time.

Then Crack! and you could see nothing for steam in the cab. I jumped back to the tender and so did Bob I was glad to see because when we sorted ourselves out to try to find what had happened we picked it out that the right hand gauge glass had 'gone' and steam and water were flying out of the top and bottom stands so that you couldn't get near. I had felt a splash but Bob having been so much nearer could have been badly scalded. I asked him was he all right and he said he was. He sounded a bit snappy as if he was annoyed and perhaps a bit scared and certainly in a hurry to get things straightened out. This sort of accident was supposed to be impossible because even when a gauge glass had broken the automatic valves ought to hold the steam and water back.

There was no time to argue about that. We had to shut two cocks in the middle of all the flying steam and water pretty quick. So I picked up the shovel and reached with it into the steam to where I guessed the handle of the top cock was. I thought that I would go for the top one first so as to stop the steam and it might then be easier to see what I was doing. On the other hand the boiler might be losing water very fast through the bottom stand and so ought not I to go for *that* one first? There are two sides to every question and this is a nuisance when there is no time to stop and sort things out.

A shovel is not really the right shape for getting behind a handle and pulling it towards you but it is at least broad enough to be a shield against the steam that's coming from where you want to place it. After a bit of scuffling I got the end of the shovel behind the handle and tried to move it by twisting the haft of the shovel. After a struggle I got the cock partly closed with the handle in a position that let me move it further by a clout with the coal-hammer.

We still had water coming out of the bottom stand but it was much easier to see what you were doing. A bit more juggling with the shovel and a tap or two with the coal-hammer closed the bottom cock and we could see where we were in the cab and after that where we were on the road. And that gave us a shock, because we had come over Wiske Moor trough while the commotion was on. I turned to the tender and tried the water-gauge. We'd got about a quarter of a tankful! We'd forgotten to look at this before we left Darlington and there we were with two good injectors but not enough water to get to York.

I told Bob and his face fell. They might not blame us for the failed injector on our own engine but there could be some nasty words about not making sure that we had enough water for the job.

Where should we stop? We were close to Northallerton by then but we could get water at Thirsk and that gave us seven or eight minutes to think things out. Bob thought we could get to York, but I didn't. I was for stopping at Thirsk whatever bother it might cause. But Bob said that if we did we couldn't hide the mistake we made at Darlington whereas with a bit of luck we could get through without anyone being any the wiser. I said that we'd not had much luck so far and he said that then it was about time we had. Anyway if there was any chance at all we'd better make the most of it. So he shut off the coach heater and eased her on the regulator.

We had another go with the tender water-gauge and tried to guess whether there was enough water for what we wanted to do. Bob looked at the boiler water. We had three-quarters of a glass. He shut the injector off and said 'Leave it off till your water is right down. Then start your feed up again and keep your water just in sight. I think we can do it, but don't let her blow off.'

I didn't think we could and I didn't want to risk losing a lead-plug by letting the boiler water get too low. What good did that do? He said that the lower you have it the less water gets carried over in the steam and so the less you waste. 'But', he said, 'when we get past Tollerton put both feeds on and fill her up or try to. If we can get by Beningbrough with plenty in the boiler, I can shut off and we can run the rest with nothing in the tank. She'll do it all right.'

I wouldn't have risked it myself. Sooner him than me. Anyway I'd do what he said. I let the boiler-water come right down and then started the left hand injector. Then it was a case of saving every drop of water. Quite different from the usual way on this train. You had a light train but plenty of everything else and you could just open her out and enjoy a fast easy run over a flat road. But on that day I hardly dared to put coal on the fire; I was afraid it might boil too much water!

Suppose Bob was wrong and our tank was empty by Tollerton. with none to spare in the boiler. What would he try to do? He would have to shut off steam right away and let the train run on to Beningbrough. He might stop there and wire for an engine to rescue us. How long would that take? Half an hour at least? The up main blocked for half an hour! Just think of the telegrams and rows that would cause!

Or might he let her run on in the hope of getting to Skelton? The would be nearer help than Beningbrough. Or might she get to Poppleton Junction? That would be better still.

I didn't say anything to him. He could sort out things like this better than I could and it wouldn't help him to have me nattering. We had passed Thirsk and so there was nothing to do but to run on and hope.

How fast should we run? Well, the faster you go the more water you use per mile. You can save water by going slow. But if you lose time you are in trouble for that. So old Bob had to decide how hard to work the engine so as not to lose more than (say) a couple of minutes to York. He had to hope that we had enough water to get through. Then he might think that if he took it easier so as to lose (say) four minutes there was a better chance that the water would last out.

This was the kind of thing to think about. He looked as if he were thinking but not more worried than usual. Perhaps he had a better idea than I had as to how much water there was in the tender. Perhaps he had a good idea as to how fast the train would need to be going past Beningbrough to carry it to the south end of York station with steam shut off. That was another point! Was it a good thing to go at full speed so that we could run a long way after shutting off? Perhaps not, because the faster you run the quicker you use water. I couldn't see how to sort that one out, and I hoped Bob felt better about it than I did. He seemed to be working her pretty easy and I thought we were not doing the speed we needed for keeping time.

I had been lucky to find the feed setting that kept the boiler water bobbing just above the bottom nut as he'd told me but I didn't like it much. It might save water but it was asking for trouble. I couldn't help checking how much water we had in the tank every couple of miles and tried to judge whether it would last to Poppleton, but I couldn't see anything to stop me from worrying. Could you rely on the gauge when the tank's nearly empty? I didn't know and I tried to tell myself that it was nothing to do with me. Bob had to do the worrying and if he *was* worrying perhaps the best thing I could do was to see every signal in case his mind was not quite on that part of the job. Not that there was much chance of finding a signal 'on'. We never used to be checked with that train but of course you could never be sure and this did seem to be a day for trouble.

The engine was steaming very well and I had to be careful to stop her from blowing off. Perhaps this running with low water in the boiler was causing it. I didn't know; it was something I'd never done before and wouldn't have done then if I hadn't been told to. Yes, she was running like a bit of silk but I thought to myself that perhaps she wouldn't have done if she'd known how near we were to a failure, and a bad failure at that. Everybody from York to Newcastle would hear about it if we stopped in the middle of a section. And that when you came to think about it was what could decide how fast to run. If you're going fast enough to run from one box to the next you need not stop in a section. So what Bob had to do was to be running fast enough at Tollerton to carry on for four miles on the level to Beningbrough with steam shut off. Had he worked this out for himself? Should I tell him this or would it upset him to poke my nose into his job at a time like that? Whether we were going as fast as that I really couldn't tell. In the ordinary way you never have any need to find out how far a train will run without steam before it actually stops. We could usually run into York from Skelton which is about three miles and have to brake to stop. Did that mean that you could run in from Beningbrough which is over five miles out? You might or you might not. If not you would probably stick on the rise from Severus to Waterworks alongside the shed where everybody could see you, but at least it would not take long to get the station pilot in front to pull you in. And anyhow if we could get plenty into the boiler by Beningbrough we could shut off there and could afford to give her steam again on the last half-mile which was where it mattered. As we were passing Alne by the time I got round to this idea, I began to think that things were not so bad after all and I opened up the feed to get the water away from that bottom nut. There was still some water showing in the tank but it was a case of touch and go.

We came by Tollerton with no sign of trouble but the boiler water was well down and so I started the other injector and guessed that that might fill her up soon after Beningbrough. Bob looked at the tank gauge and there was hardly anything showing. He looked at me and I looked at him but didn't say anything. There was nothing to do but hold your breath. Could we get to Beningbrough before the water finished? We just looked ahead and hoped. For three minutes we just stood and let things happen. The boiler water got up to a good half-glass and Bob evidently decided that that would do as he shut off his injector.

We passed Beningbrough distant and we knew we were nearly home. We looked ahead, hoping for the best, and it seemed to take a long time to get to the station although we were running at nearly the ordinary speed. We passed under the bridge, passed the railway cottages, and we were just coming to the next bridge when steam started to blow out of the left hand overflow. I shut the injector off, Bob shut the regulator and on we went without steam. We'd got no water in the tank, but more than half a boiler-full and if we got no board against us we were pretty sure we could get to the south end of York Number 8.

There was nothing to do but look ahead and notice how we were slowing down. I wished the wind were behind us. I thought that a heavier train would hold the speed better than we were doing. On the other hand with a heavier train we would not have got so far. But she kept going, a bit slow past Poppleton and noticeably slow at Severus. Then the curve and the gradient really slowed us down and we came creeping up past the shed but Bob could afford to give her some steam to keep her moving over the crossings and under the roof. He let her roll to a slow stop under the water crane. We were late, but just to make sure Bob got back up the tender and I dropped the bag to him and turned the water on to get a drop into the tank while we were hooking off. It was a bit fussy when we had half a boiler of water but we couldn't resist a water-crane after the half hour of worry we'd just had.

NOT SO PACIFIC

When somebody told you (said the driver) that they were
building new engines nearly twice as big as a Z you didn't know
what to think about it. A Z could take eighteen coaches from
York to Darlington in 50 minutes so what more did they want?
Did they want to do it in 40 minutes or did they want to run
thirty-coach trains? And did they think that a bigger engine
was bound to be better than a Z? You could kill a fireman on a
Z if you thrashed her for half an hour, so what's the good of
building anything bigger? They built an electric engine for
expresses between York and Newcastle but they never put any
wires up to run it with. Did they know what they were trying
to do with their Pacifics or whatever they called them?

One of my mates said he'd heard that the Great Northern had
built a couple of Pacifics and he thought that our lot were doing
the same just to stop the Great Northern from being one-up on
us. Well, you wouldn't think that they would be such big kids
as that, but then you never know. First an electric with no
electricity to run it and then a monster that's sure to be too long
for some of the curves. They just go out of their way to look for
trouble, as if it didn't come fast enough on its own. Always
playing about with something different and just beating themselves with it. Look at the S they fitted up with cylinders nearly
as big as the boiler. The Stump they called it, or something like
that. Never a bit of good. They always have to be making things
bigger and they get worse every time.

Everybody knew that the railways were going to be sorted out
and joined up in groups. This meant that the North Eastern
would finish at the end of 1922. We heard that at Darlington they
were rushing the new engines a bit so as to get one or two out
before the end of the year. They managed it and rumours came
round of an engine on eighteen wheels and as long as the biggest
coaches. Nobody believed that and presently the news came that
it was the engine and tender that had eighteen wheels between
them. The engine, they said, was like a long fat Z with a firebox
about twice as wide as on the Z. It had six driving wheels and

2. No 695 (Class W). Built for Scarborough-Whitby line

3. No 1352 (Class X). Three-cylinder engine for hump-shunting. Note single slide-bar

4. No 1113 (Class Y). Three-cylinder engine for goods service

5. No 2163 (Class Z). One of the later batches. The earlier ones had brass-rimmed chimneys and safety-valves as in Class VI

46. No 1619 (Class 3CC). Three-cylinder compound
47. No 730 (Class 4CC). Four-cylinder compound. Belpaire firebox. Midland
    style front lookouts
48. No 2400 (Class 4-6-2). Three-cylinder engine. Three pop safety-valves

three cylinders. Pity they couldn't have worked a few more in while they were at it!

From the beginning of 1923 our railway, the old North Eastern, was part of the London & North Eastern Railway. It was the North Eastern part or section or division of the LNER but it was a long time before it made any difference to the enginemen. All the paperwork was marked LNER fairly soon but nothing else changed for months.

They got the second new engine out early in 1923 and they painted the usual North Eastern name on the tender. We used to see these new engines running light or with slow trains now and again on the usual running-in turns from Darlington. We heard rumours that they had to go back to the works for things to be altered and I suppose this always happens with new engines. All sorts of rumours came through. The engines were 'not bad', 'could be better', 'no good', 'failures', 'should be all right when they get run in' but nobody had heard that they were twice as good as a Z or anything like that. But everybody said that they burned a lot of coal. No wonder! As they were a lot bigger than a Z they were bound to need a lot of steam to move themselves, let alone a train, and so they were bound to burn more coal. You could be sure that firemen were not going to like them. All the same they gradually got on to regular passenger trains and each engine had its own driver. And, would you believe it?—they gave one to me and told me to do my best with it.

What does doing your best mean in a case like this? Best for who? The Railway company? Or the fireman? Or me? Or who? You've got a lot of things to think about when you're in a position like that. If you get all you can out of a big new engine nicely broken in, all the high-ups will be delighted and will expect every engineman to do the same on every trip. What are the other men in a link going to think about anybody who sets a pace that nobody else can keep up? What sort of a life would they give him? No, you just can't take the risk of bashing a big engine even once if you want a quiet life. An engineman likes a big engine only if it makes the job easier for him; it is better for him if no one else knows how hard the engine can work when you really press it. So a driver who has any thought for his fireman never pushes a big engine. He makes sure not to pick up any time even if he has only three coaches behind him. There is nothing in the rule-book to tell him to go faster than the working time-table says and if he is anything like a good union man he won't do it. In fact if he holds his union in any respect at all he daren't do it.

But anyway when I'd had a look around the engine with my mate I could see she was no good. The boiler was a long sausage (five lagging bands on the barrel). What sort of a 'jimmy' was going to be needed on the blast-pipe to get a draught through that lot? And you would need some draught to get a hot fire in a box of that size. It was a lot wider than any we'd ever had on the North Eastern and I could see that my mate was going to have some bother in getting coal into the back corners. It was twice as wide as the box on a Z but it was not so long. Still there were a lot more fire-bars to keep covered and I thought that before I could really open her out I would need two firemen.

But when I looked at her length I wondered how we were going to get her out of the shed. She was far too long to go round any sort of curve. Still somebody had got her in so I supposed I should be able to get her out.

So I got on to oiling round. I must say that the motion was no worse to get at than it is on a Z, but that's bad enough. There were two extra coupling rod ends to look after and a bit more brake gear. In the cab it was not a lot different from a Z except that the boiler was higher and you couldn't see much out of the front window.

I wasn't looking forward to running this engine, I can tell you, but I supposed that somebody would have to do it. I certainly wasn't going to rush. Even at that she groaned at every point and curve in the yard and on the way to Newcastle Central. She might be all right when she got on to a bit of straight going but till then I wasn't taking any chances.

The first time I took her out of Central we were going to York with ten on. I was a bit nervous with a big engine that was new to me, a stiff regulator, and quite a few people watching. I set the sand running right from the start and she didn't slip, but she creaked and groaned as if she might and so I just kept her going over the bridge. I didn't know how she would take the bend at the far end and so I was not going to hit it too fast. I had the feeling—and I never got over it—that 2401 didn't like this bit of road. There's no point in hurrying anyway. It's impossible to start fast from Central with all the train on a curve. If you've any sense you won't run a long engine fast at the bend at the other end of the bridge. If you are worrying as to whether the bridge is strong enough to carry all the weight of a big engine, all you can do is to take it very steady. A driver has to think about safety before everything else. So I never rushed any Pacific over King Edward Bridge, and to tell the truth I never felt much like rushing anywhere. There's too much of it done these days and it gets you nowhere.

So on my first trip I didn't open her out until we had got well onto the straight, and then she picked up all right. In fact, by the time we'd got past Bensham she was going a bit too fast and so I eased off. It's no use running before time anywhere on the North Eastern because if you do you'll always find signals against you. I've always found that if you are a couple of minutes late you get on a lot better.

I asked my mate how she was going and he said he thought she was all right. We had 180 pounds of steam on the gauge and the red mark was at 200. She had three safety valves which made me think that somebody wasn't sure whether the boiler was really strong enough and so I never pushed my mate to get any Pacific to blow off. Not that he would have done it anyway. I think he didn't believe that the boiler was safe and so he never tried to get enough steam to blow off. I don't think that 2401 blew off more than once a month. We must have saved a lot of coal that way, besides what I saved by never pushing any engine hard. It doesn't do them any good. Everybody knows that and everybody knows that any driver who picks up time does it by thrashing the engine. It isn't worth it and I never did it. Better to be a minute or two late than to run the risk of overworking the fireman and wearing the engine out.

So we pottered up to Durham where we were booked to stop, just about keeping time. There didn't seem to be much life in the engine but she did it all right. When we stopped, the station inspector came up and said he supposed that with such a big engine we would not need the banker up to Relly Mill. I soon put him right on that. There was a banking engine at Durham for pushing trains up to Relly Mill and I wasn't going to start without it. Not me! Did he think I was going up that bank with an engine I didn't know and no push behind the train? No fear! Supposing we stuck? Whose fault would it be then? And anyway you can't afford to let them get away with anything. Once let them get the idea that Pacifics don't need bankers and the next thing will be that Zs don't need bankers and before you know where you are there would be no bankers for anything. There's more in engine-driving than just driving engines. You've got to look after your own job and you've not got to do anything that might cause anyone else to lose his.

So off we went with the banker behind the train, letting him do most of the pushing as usual. This is only right. After all, banking engines spend most of their time standing and so they ought to work hard when they *are* working.

My mate had put plenty of coal on the fire while we were standing and shut the door tight as we got away so that we turned out plenty of smoke. This makes a lot of people think that both the engine and the fireman are working hard and so to them at least you look as if you are trying.

On to Darlington we ran all right, nothing startling, about like a pretty fair Z would have done and we got in about a minute late. The station staff managed to save that minute and so we started for York on time. Most trains were booked pretty fast on this stretch and Zs could do it all right. I had been told that the Pacifics were all right but I didn't really believe it. To me they looked too big to be fast or to be safe if they could go fast and when we got going I felt that I was right. I got her up to the right speed for keeping time or perhaps dropping a minute or two but I didn't think she liked it. She rode all right but then it was a good road and you could expect any engine that wasn't run down to ride well on it. But what was an engine of that weight doing to the track at 70 miles an hour? The more I thought about it, the less I liked it. I supposed that the permanent-way people would find out in time what the track was suffering under Pacifics flying up and down between Darlington and York but till then I wasn't taking any chances. It was bad enough to have to do about seventy just to keep time, but I wasn't going to run any faster than that. Better to be safe than sorry. Better to drop a couple of minutes than to have a box or a big end or an eccentric running hot. Perhaps in a month or two I might get more confident and would risk the speed needed for running on time, but not at first!

But, you know, I never got past that first feeling. I was sure that 2401 herself didn't like speed. I can't explain it but when you've been firing and driving engines for thirty years you can *feel* what is good and what is bad for an engine. I was never happy about 2401. She *could* pull but she didn't like it. I believe that she might have run fast, but I never dared to try her. At seventy she rode and shook in a queer way (at least I found she did but other drivers said they didn't notice anything) and I felt that this was just a bit too fast for her. So whatever size of train we had I never aimed to do Darlington to York in less than forty-seven minutes. Never mind what the working time-table said. Anybody can write figures down, but it's the practical men on the job who know what's sensible and what isn't.

So we went down through Northallerton and Thirsk, nice and steady. My mate seemed to be putting plenty on the fire and keeping her up to about 180 and I was sniffing for hot boxes all the time but nothing went wrong. We had only dropped a couple of minutes by Beningbrough, but we should lose a bit more in running round the bends from Severus Junction in to York. I couldn't really forget the length of this engine with that sausage of a boiler stuck out in front of me and so I had let the speed get well down by Poppleton Junction and just touched the brakes at Severus to get a bit of back-pull from the train on the first curve. But I took no chance over the crossing, or round the bend of Number 8 at York. I didn't want the front buffer-beam to scatter any coping stones by being forced outwards through going too fast. So we crept in gently, losing a bit of time but keeping out of trouble.

And that's how I always felt with 2401. She could do the work but I felt she was right at her limit and that she would get herself into some sort of trouble—I couldn't say what—if I let her use all her strength in pulling or running. Some other men would let her go as if she were a Z, and got by without too much trouble, but I never did. I was sure before I ever saw one that the Pacifics were too big and I never found anything to make me change my mind about it.

Of course I had inspectors riding with me now and again and of course they usually wanted me to work the engine harder than I was doing. When they did I always said that they could run her themselves any way they liked, but they never did. Eventually they left me to go my own way and as time went on other drivers found that it did not pay to keep pushing Pacifics hard. Now and again perhaps, but not all the time.

I suppose a lot of passengers must have thought that the Pacifics were big enough to pull anything or to run an ordinary train at a hundred miles an hour. When they didn't, some of them were probably disappointed and felt that they hadn't been getting their moneysworth. I remember one day when I was running 2401 from Newcastle to York, a passenger came up to us after we stopped at Darlington and asked me whether there was anything wrong with the engine. I might have asked him whether there was anything right with her but you have to be careful what you say to strangers as you never know whether they are high-up company officials. So I told him that I couldn't hold her in and repeated it. I just couldn't hold her in. I don't know what he made of it, but it left me pretty well in the clear. I wasn't blaming the engine for not keeping time and I wasn't admitting that I was deliberately doing wrong but at the worst had only misjudged my timing of the train.

One thing I was sure of and that was that no remarks from passengers were ever going to make me run an engine in any way but my own. So we went at our usual speed from Darlington to York dropping a couple of minutes.

I was always careful not to push 2401 hard anywhere, but even so she got hot trailing axle-boxes. In time they altered her to have outside trailing boxes as she ought to have had from the start. The Zs had always had them, so why did they want to change? But then, why did they build Pacifics at all for the North Eastern? They could never have expected them to beat the Zs which were plenty big enough, and they never did for any length of time. Certainly while I had 2401 she never did any more than a decent Z could have done.

CHAPTER II

NORTH EASTERN SPECTATOR

NEARLY everyone who started his railway-enthusiasm near the zenith of British railway development round about the time of World War I did so on the basis of personal observation in the vicinity of his home. Information about doings further afield was provided by the *Railway Magazine* and *The Locomotive* and at holiday times the enthusiast used his presence in a part of the country new to him to examine the working of trains in it. What excited his primary interest was the strange magic of the steam locomotive. The interest spread in greater or lesser degree to associated phases of railway operation, for example, signalling, or civil engineering, and inevitably into the history of locomotives and railways. 'History is bunk' according to Henry Ford, and whilst not everyone agrees with this even with the aid of wide interpretation of the word 'bunk', few would claim that history, however dramatically expounded, is so vivid as was the sight, sound and scent of a steam locomotive vigorously doing its stuff.

This book is not intended as a 'history of North Eastern locomotives' although it is concerned with the past and with North Eastern locomotives. Naturally, many 'facts' of history already published in officially-based histories, are repeated (but not necessarily endorsed) in what is intended to be convenient form, but the main aim is to present the picture of North Eastern steam seen by an interested observer who looked because he liked doing it and not because he was obliged—or felt obliged—to do so for any more material purpose. So this account is somewhat 'personal' but its justification is not any assumption that the particular per-son's acquaintance with North Eastern locomotives was made in any very unusual way. On the contrary, it probably represented the average enthusiast's awakening of intelligent interest in steam locomotives and the running of railway trains. Most readers prefer what comfortably lines up with their own experiences to anything that appears to conflict with them or with established beliefs. Perhaps for that reason many enthusiasts like to read personal reminiscences about railways, or perhaps it is because such reminiscences are among the few remaining novelties about steam on railways.

My first sight of North Eastern locomotives was at Leeds (New) and they included one of the notable Class R1 4-4-0s. At the same place later on I saw one of the magnificent 3-cylinder Atlantics of Class Z. These were rare occasions because although I lived in the North Western/L & Y sector of the West Riding it was unusual for me to go to Leeds. But even in a single short visit to a station containing steam locomotives that the visitor knew only from literature and pictures if at all, he could be surprised by all sorts of details in the running of the engines and of the trains.

A very noticeable difference between the working of North Eastern locomotives and of those that I already knew was the performance of the Westinghouse pump. A prolonged session of 'snort-snort-snort' seemed to me a frightful fuss to make about the essentially undramatic operation of taking the brakes off. Even more irritating were the fitful sniffs from the pump in making up for air leakage on an engine that was standing still and doing nothing. I should have thought that the driver would shut the pump off for the sake of peace and quietness, but it seemed that the North Eastern enginemen took as little notice of these restless stirrings as diesel crews take of the thunderous bumblings in the tin box behind them. Perhaps the noise helped to keep them awake in warm weather. Perhaps the noise was less of a nuisance than the struggle to get the mechanism going again after a rest.

A driver's application of the Westinghouse brake was accompanied by a much fiercer flow of air than the corresponding inrush with the vacuum brake and the difference in sound heard on a station-platform, let alone on the footplate, was acutely noticeable.

My acquaintance with North Eastern steam at speed began after I had found cycling to be an agreeable pastime. It opened to me hundreds of square miles of previously inaccessible areas and added to life a number of dimensions, one of which was North Eastern steam. Many years elapsed before I began to realise that the bicycle had similarly widened the horizons of many railway enthusiasts before World War I. After World War II, extensive rail-travel by juvenile 'spotters' suggested that many more people could afford to travel by train than was formerly the case.

The industrial area of the West Riding was too hilly for continuously comfortable cycling and the outlook was grim rather than picturesque, but to the east things got easier on the legs and on the eye. To the north east, in addition, one encountered the North Eastern Railway. It was only the southern fringe of that railway, far away from its coal-mining origin in Durham, and to that extent untypical, but it provided live interest different in form and colour from what the North Western or the Lancashire & Yorkshire presented. Moreover it included York, that (almost) unique railway centre now reduced, like British railways themselves, to a fraction of its former self. One must be thankful for pictures and memories.

A strange fact that is a source of perennial regret to me is that for some years I never made any note of my observations of locomotives or their work. This may be specially surprising to the 'spotters' of post World War II and it may be associated with the fact that earlier generations of schoolboys were markedly derisive of those of their number who showed more than passing interest in locomotives. It was regarded as a sign of arrested development; engine-watching was for infants only. Indeed for years after I had left that stage I met few people who had such interest or at least would admit to such interest. The austere pages of the *Railway Magazine* made it clear that there was a fair volume of non-professional interest in railways and their work, but it was impressively solemn and portentous; only by extending one's imagination in respect of faint hints here and there could one come to believe that many schoolboys knew or cared much about locomotives.

On the old road from London to York was the station at Burton Salmon where the L &Y route from York to Manchester diverged from the Midland route from York to Sheffield. There were platforms for the two most easterly tracks and the station name-boards had salmon-coloured backgrounds. I eventually decided that this was just a coincidence; the same colour was similarly used at other North Eastern stations.

At Burton Salmon the North Eastern engines were to me more interesting than those of the other railways represented there. In particular I saw, more than once, a 'fitted freight' train brought from the York direction by a North Eastern 4–6–0 with smallish driving wheels and I cannot now be sure whether it was of Class S or Class S2. (Had I been a 'spotter' and had retained my note, I could have settled this question.) It was certainly the most impressive-looking locomotive I saw there and so it was probably the larger S2.

It happened that it was at Burton Salmon that I saw, in 1941, what would have been incredible two years earlier, an A4 streamlined Pacific in charge of a miscellaneous goods train. During World War II the railways had to take not only military traffic and goods for the war effort but also a large proportion of the goods traffic that would in normal times have gone by road, and any engine that could turn a wheel in spite of prolonged neglect might be used for any kind of train. World War I never laid such stress on the railways. Locomotives continued to be kept clean and North Eastern steam, green and brassy, was as bright as any.

Burton Salmon was a pleasant train-watching spot, the aspect in every direction being rural without a blemish and so it remains except that the chimneys and cooling towers of Ferrybridge power station overtop the woods to the south, that Eggborough looms similarly five miles away to the south east and that the eastern horizon is dominated by the big tower of record-breaking Drax ten miles away.

Three and a half-miles north of Burton Salmon the Roman road from London to York is bridged by the Leeds–Selby line of the North Eastern at South Milford, near the bottom of a six-mile drop at about 1 in 150 to the plain of York and Gascoigne Wood. Eastbound passenger trains commonly flew over the bridge at a stirring pace, mostly in charge of gleaming green 4–4–0s of Classes Q and R. In sombre black, but no less fleet, North Western engines were to be seen on the Liverpool–Hull through trains. North Eastern 0–6–0s and 0–8–0s with westbound goods trains slogged noisily over this bridge. Down the bank they came cautiously and it was interesting to judge from the numbers of 'buffered-up' vehicles how much of the train was being held back by the engine and tender and how much was being restrained by the brake-van.

Two miles further north the Roman road runs under that part of the Leeds–York line which lies between Micklefield and Church Fenton, the six mile Church Fenton bank at an average of about 1 in 150. It crosses the road by a high bridge in about a mile of embankment, splendidly visible from the road near the Ash Tree Inn on the edge of the village of Barkston Ash. Passenger trains normally ran very fast down this bank and it was natural to want to time them.

The first thought was to time an observed number of up and down movements of the engine's coupling rod. The second thought was to count the number of such movements in a pre-determined period. The third thought was to fix that period so that the number of revolutions was equal to the speed in miles per hour. On this basis, the timing period in seconds is equal to the diameter of the driving wheels in inches, divided by 5.6 and so it is only about 14 seconds. This is not too bad if you have a watch with a centre-seconds hand and especially if it has a stop-watch mechanism so that you can at least start the hand on the timing period without looking at the watch. But I had none of these things and I found it impossible to be certain of counting the revolutions reliably when they were coming at me five or six times per second.

So I thought it might be better to time over the longest

distance that could be readily distinguished and to calculate the speed by division. Thinking about this on site, the telegraph poles at once suggested themselves as timing points and the next question was 'How far apart are they?' The only reliable way of finding this out was to measure it myself, but of course the general public were not permitted to be on the railway even for such a harmless purpose as measuring the pitch of telegraph posts. And anyway a foot-rule was a bit short for measuring such a distance.

I might have borrowed a surveyor's chain if I had known anyone who possessed one and was willing to lend it, but it would form an awkward parcel to carry by bicycle and would be laborious to use over any distance long enough to form a reliable basis for timing.

Then remembering that a good method of timing a train when you are in it is to use rail-lengths for measuring distance, I realised that the track itself forms its own measuring device. If I could count the number of rail lengths between two readily identifiable telegraph posts, my problem was solved, provided of course that I knew the length of the rail. I was pretty sure that this would be either 30 ft or 45 ft. A remote chance was that it might be 60 ft, which was standard on the London & North Western Railway but on no other British railway at that time.

If one stands far enough from a railway embankment to be able to see the side of the nearest rail, one is too far away for fishplates to be distinguished with certainty. So it seemed impossible to use the rail-joint scheme for measuring a length without going on to the permanent way and walking about a mile while high in the air and visible to all and sundry for some ten minutes. But the 'all and sundry' are not numerous very early on a Sunday morning. Moreover having reached the site by bicycle it would be worth some effort to get the bicycle on the track when with any luck about the condition of the cinders alongside the ballast, one might cover a mile in much less than ten minutes. Furthermore, a cyclometer fitted to the bicycle would provide an independent check on the distance.

Railway track was about the only part of Britain on which the mere act of trespassing was specifically illegal and the railways had gone to enormous trouble to prevent anyone from making himself vulnerable in this respect by accidentally getting on to the permanent way. Only those who have tried to do this know how difficult it is and of them probably only a small proportion know how much harder the task is if it includes the additional importation of a bicycle. So I spent some time over a preliminary survey of possible routes for reaching the track on the Leeds side of the bridge and of leaving it about a mile away on the other side of it. (I resolved to have the advantage of the gradient on this journey.) Cart tracks were handy for both entry and exit, although in the latter case they led past habitations with always the chance that some damned dog would waken everybody if it heard a noise at an unusual hour. It might be better to re-trace the measured length in the opposite direction so as to avoid close approach to any house.

This was to be done in high summer so that there was enough light to make the operation possible well before anyone could be expected to be about, although in the country some people tend to get up early for not quite legitimate purposes and police sometimes get up early enough to catch them. While thus engaged a policeman might well be interested at the sight of a cyclist on a railway embankment at 6.00 a.m. So the whole scheme was really asking for trouble and the object was clearly not worth it. But sheer perversity and a liking for being out in the very quiet hours between them persuaded me to do the job.

The morning was a miracle of peace and beauty, everything worked as planned and an hour later I thanked the North Eastern Railway for raising no objection by buying from its York refreshment room one of the nicest cups of tea it has ever provided.

I determined that from the sixth telegraph pole on the west side of the road-bridge to another bridge over a cart-track to the east of it was 0.59 miles or from the same pole to a third bridge, not easily distinguishable in poor light, was 0.81 miles. From the road-bridge to the next bridge was 0.37 miles. So there were three convenient timing-lengths appropriate for different degrees of visibility. I also ascertained as a by-product that the nominal spacing of the telegraph post was three chains.

And what information did I obtain from my 'measured mile'? Downhill speeds of passenger trains were commonly about 70 mph and the fastest train I timed was doing slightly over 80 behind a Class R 4-4-0. More thrilling because of the flailing connecting rod at higher rotational speed was a Class S2 4-6-0 doing about 75.

In such a location none of these speeds is a demonstration of any notable locomotive power and indeed in most cases the engine was running without steam. Down a gradient of 1 in 150 a train of bogie coaches can be kept going at 75 mph by gravity alone. Once having brought the train up to that speed the engine needs only enough steam to overcome its own frictional resistances. There was no object in going much faster as the curve on the approach to Church Fenton station at the bottom of the bank, although well superelevated, is not wisely taken at much over 75 mph, and the natural drifting speed of an average passenger train and locomotive down the bank was nicely inside this limit.

Whilst riding down this bank in the first coach of a train behind a Class Z Atlantic, I noted that we were running at slightly over 70 mph without steam. As we approached Church Fenton the driver opened the regulator and immediately the 'whirr' of the coach-wheels was markedly reduced. It seemed to me that, under compression between the rest of the train and the locomotive, the first coach had become skewed to the track, the flanges of the wheels of the leading bogie bearing laterally on one rail while the trailing bogie similarly pressed on the other rail. As soon as the engine began to pull, the coach was straightened out and the flange-pressure reduced.

But running conditions down the Church Fenton bank were not always so smooth as the passenger might imagine. I retain a most vivid impression, gained from the overbridge at Church Fenton, of violent lateral oscillation of the tender behind a Class Q 4-4-0 at the head of a passenger train running quite fast round the curve. The tender was by far the liveliest vehicle in the train and perhaps I ought not to have been surprised as a rather elemental six-wheeler, with water slopping about inside it, has no special reason to be docile with no drawbar-pull at high speed.

Church Fenton station, with four through platforms and a bay, was an impressive rural junction, the more so because of the North Eastern habit of providing a profusion of signals. This was obvious even to the most juvenile eye that had seen much of other railways. To me, 'brought up', so to speak, on the North Western which made all it needed itself, the North Eastern's purchase of signals from a private firm which cast its name very firmly on counterweights and the like, was very striking. I immediately formed the impression that the railway company had handed over the entire signalling problem to the contractor who had put in every installation as many signals as he thought his client would stand for, irrespective of technical need!

Each North Eastern signal post was topped by a finial to finish all finials, a four-foot spear rampant on a flattened half-onion. The contrast between this and the North Western's modest wooden cap in the shape of a barely distinguishable pyramid was complete. A bit of pointless fuss in North Eastern signalling was that every 'calling-on' arm was lowered with the associated main arm instead of having its movement limited as usual to 'calling-on'.

One had time (but not much) to muse on such matters between train movements at Church Fenton and to note a corresponding fussiness in decorative detail of North Eastern locomotives in comparison with the Midland, Great Central and L & Y locomotives that regularly went past. A brass ring round the boiler barrel at its junction with the smokebox was noticeable in this connection. I felt sure that the North Eastern double side-window cab was a 'good thing' and so was its upward opening flat ventilator in the roof, but even so, North Eastern men hung themselves more noticeably outside the cab in hot weather than did the occupants of the airier shelters on other companies' locomotives.

The four-track route between York and Church Fenton was the scene of occasional 'races' between passenger trains of different ownership. During periods when southbound trains were booked to leave York simultaneously such contests might happen daily. Whether they did or not depended on the personalities and moods of the engine drivers. In most cases they were quite indifferent as to whether they were 'passed' or not and what may have seemed to passengers to be races may not have been anything of the sort. Leeds-bound trains had the advantage that they could run through Church Fenton without slackening speed, whereas a wriggle in the other line between the large signal box and the easternmost platform was a bit violent at anything over a mile-a-minute and so often demanded a marked 'easing' of the engine. So a train on the Normanton line had to have a good lead in the approach to Church Fenton if it was to pass under the road before its rival did so. North Eastern engines were rarely beaten on this stretch if really trying, by any competitor with an equal load.

At Church Fenton one could be impressed by the length of goods trains that were handled by the little o-6-os of Class C1. This was the case on flat routes such as York to Gascoigne Wood marshalling sidings near South Milford. But the same engines were restricted to much smaller loads up the bank to Micklefield and indeed o-8-os of Classes T1 and T2 commonly handled the goods trains in that direction.

Towards York on the four-track line from Church Fenton the first station was Ulleskelf, a rather jumbled village on the right bank of the Wharfe. It was, and still is, a centre for fishermen. The station was limited to an island platform between the Sheffield lines, and a goods yard, but from a distance the profusion of signals suggested a much more elaborate layout.

From Ulleskelf to the next station, Bolton Percy, is about one and a quarter miles. Because of the intervening River Wharfe the distance by public road between the villages is about seven miles and so one may suspect a fair amount of unauthorised walking on the railway track over the river-bridge during the hours of darkness.

Cycling in this region in the deep peace of the countryside one still September evening I paused on the bridge at Bolton Percy with the possibility in mind of seeing some train—or at least its lights—pass by. Presently from the south came the sound of a running train; it gradually died and was followed by noises as of a locomotive standing in a station. Doors banged and then the engine started off with clear, distinct accelerating beats from a chimney that was coming towards me. Obviously the train had left Ulleskelf and would soon come into sight. But it did not appear. After a time steam was shut off and the running sound of the coaches gradually died as the train came to rest but still with no visible sign. Why should it stop between Ulleskelf and Bolton Percy? Again a door banged. Again the engine started, a hundred yards away by ear, but quite invisible, and its quickening and strengthening beats coming out of nowhere were unnervingly uncanny. What was it all about? After some tense moments a headlight appeared at a bend in a cutting over a quarter of a mile away while the exhaust beat seemed to be made only 50 yards from my feet. Then I realised that the second start had been from Ulleskelf; the first one I heard had been from Church Fenton station, three miles to the south. The combination of a dead-calm evening and the hearty blast of a Class R1 4-4-0 had led me into a ludicrous underestimate of distance.

Bolton Percy was then a tiny village, in itself hardly justifying a station. But when it was built, country people thought nothing of walking three miles or so to join a train or whatever other kind of conveyance there might be and horsedrawn farm vehicles commonly covered much greater distances in fetching or delivering materials. So although Bolton Percy was small its station had a goods yard serving many square miles of country, and moreover a siding raised over five recesses into which road vehicles could be backed to receive coal from bottom-door railway wagons. On many such North Eastern installations, the loading points were labelled with the names of different collieries and railway wagons also carrying their colliery-owners' names were placed accordingly. At Bolton Percy the raised track remained long after it had ceased to be used and as late as 1969 there remained in position the notice

'ENGINES ARE ALLOWED TO USE THESE DEPOTS'

in marked contradistinction to the far commoner notices prohibiting the passage of locomotives into sidings.

Nearer York is a very convenient site for measuring the speed
of trains on this level track. Colton Bridge, carrying a public
road, is rather less than half a mile from a bridge leading to
Brumber Hill Farm and the Ordnance Survey enables one to
decide that the separation of the bridges is 0.44 mile. With a
stop-watch, timing over this length is easy. A train could in fact
be timed even if hidden by trains on parallel tracks, by noting
the instants of coincidence of exhaust jet and bridges. Although
there was plenty of traffic over this length speed was rarely
excitingly high. A mile a minute was usual and a 'race' might
produce 65 to 70 mph. North Eastern locomotives were neither
distinguished nor disgraced in any such comparison. My 'record'
was about 75 mph by a Great Central rebuilt D9 4-4-0 in charge
of a short unidentified passenger train on a Sunday afternoon.
One appreciated such gaiety as this but one was frequently
reminded by Class T2 0-8-0s pounding along at 25 mph with
long trains of wagons that goods rather than gaiety kept the
railways going.

In the *Railway Magazine* for May 1921 Mr. C. J. Allen reported
an incident in which a recently rebuilt Lancashire & Yorkshire
four-cylinder 4-6-0 with a trivial load of 130 tons decisively beat
a more heavily loaded North Eastern Class R 4-4-0 in running
from York to Church Fenton. This was regarded at Horwich as
a feather in the cap, although it had no technical significance. It
is not the only suggestion that professional locomotive engineers
could be almost as emotional as the veriest amateur over a visible
race on the railway.

Examples of every class of North Eastern main-line locomotive
could be seen on this stretch running trains between York and
Leeds. The Newcastle-York-Leeds-Harrogate-Northallerton-
Newcastle loop was a favourite 'diagram' for locomotives
stationed at York, Newcastle and Leeds. Because of the two
bridges over the Tyne at Newcastle an engine might repeat its
daily duty indefinitely without using a turntable.

The two remarkable Class Q1 4-4-0s were occasionally to be

seen on the York-Leeds line. With their gigantic coupled wheels, proudly-set boiler and clerestory cab-roof they were distinctive machines, striding majestically along with trains of five or six coaches.

An entirely different impression was created by the biggest North Eastern engines, the 'Pacifics' built just before the grouping of railways in 1923. I saw one of them amble past Colton Bridge in a reluctant way with a Leeds-York train. To the eye it was a long heavy monster that had been given a light job, well within the scope of a Class Q 4-4-0, so as to leave a bit more elbow-room ·in the shed. This class of locomotive, like the Great Western 'Great Bear' 14 years older, seemed to have been built as a gesture rather than as a serious attempt to meet any operational need. I should have liked to see it demonstrating its up-to-date power and speed by hurtling along a level line at 90 mph, but no North Eastern train ever needed such a speed to keep to its booked schedule and no North Eastern 'Pacific' ever showed such sparkle anywhere.

I remember Copmanthorpe station particularly because for a time a petrol-engined rail-coach maintained a shuttle service between there, York, Earswick and Strensall. Chaloner Whin junction, on the way, was an impressively signalled place with three double cross-overs between the Leeds and the Normanton/Sheffield lines. (The latter were officially called 'Normanton' lines but 'Sheffield' is an equally informative designation with the advantage that the position of Sheffield is more widely known than that of Normanton.)

Observation at Chaloner Whin was easy, for the four tracks were spanned by a little-used road on a bridge of riveted steel plates with webs and top flanges wide enough to provide useful shelter against rain that came down in any direction with a horizontal component parallel to the rails. From all four brick pillars, there extended along the road three-bar railings offering unobstructed views and rather sharp-edged seats. Rail traffic here offered varied entertainment and reasonably fast running by passenger trains coming in from Church Fenton. At Chaloner Whin one might see regularly very diverse forms of 'Atlantic' from Horwich and Doncaster and another quite different set of four classes of North Eastern 'Atlantic'. Mostly, however, one saw long goods trains taken along by chugging 0-8-0s and 0-6-0s and one could appreciate the difficulties to be overcome by the men in the big signal-box in keeping these trains moving well enough to leave clear paths for the passenger trains.

There is no signal box and no signal now at Chaloner Whin but the colour-light signals a quarter of a mile away alongside the Leeds and Normanton lines are (or used to be) provided with loud-speakers by which the area-controller in York Station might waken enginemen who had fallen asleep whilst waiting for a long time for a signal light to change from red to something else. In earlier days this was done by the rattle of the mechanism of a semaphore signal, rapidly oscillated by the signalman for the purpose.

Although goods trains could all be kept clear of the passenger station at York in the days when it was limited to fourteen platforms, it suffered traffic problems that fascinated the observer even more than they harassed the operating staff. With the four main tracks through the station signalled for both directions of running and with tracks laid out to let anything go from anywhere to anywhere else there were forests of spiked and slotted signals with incessantly waving arms. North Eastern steam did a lot of the work here, but not all. Engines of the Great Northern, Great Eastern, Great Central, Midland and Lancashire & Yorkshire railways were also regular visitors to York but none was more splendid than the North Eastern's own Class Z 'Atlantic'. Only the Great Northern 'large Atlantics' might challenge their slightly gay magnificence if not their ability, in skilled and patient hands, to get very heavy trains away from Platform 14. With steam sanders in good order, an easily-worked regulator and a driver who knew that nothing was to be gained by trying to hurry, a Class Z 'Atlantic' had less difficulty than may be imagined by those who remember only the frightful efforts made by 'Pacifics' in the bad condition that became common during World War II and immediately after it. But with all admiration for the men who got the 'Atlantics' to do the job beautifully and for those who manfully tried to make run-down 'Pacifics' to do it at all, one must remember that a helping push at the rear end of the train from one of the o-6-oT 'station pilots' would have moved a heavy train out with no hesitation and at least twice as fast. One must ascribe official refusal to adopt this artifice to a strange fear that once a shunting engine gets to work at the back of a train, the driver of the engine at the front will not be able to stop it from being pushed into danger.

York Station itself was so well known to every locomotive enthusiast through personal observation or through extensive literature that little need be written about it here. It was at the southern end of perhaps the most famous railway race-course in Great Britain, the 44 mile stretch from Darlington across part of the Plain of York. With only slight curves (except at York) and only slight gradients it was (and is) ideal for fast running and its rural surroundings do nothing to diminish its attraction for either a train-rider or a line-side observer. Like the Swindon-Didcot part of the Great Western, which also lies in a named 'Vale', the North Eastern's race-track is overlooked by a white horse on a hill-side—that at Kilburn.

The curvature of the platform lines at York created difficulties in the starting of north-bound trains, but once clear of the platform a down gradient compensates for the resistance of the S-curve to Severus Junction, where the real straight begins. At that junction, the line from the passenger station runs parallel to the less sharply-curved goods lines that extend from Holgate Bridge and lie to the west of the station and the engine-shed alongside extensive sidings. The name of the junction was more probably based on Roman association with York than on any reflection on the fact that goods trains were habitually severed and sorted in its vicinity. In the course of rationalization of many North Eastern matters, the LNER re-named the junction signal box as York Yard North. This is more informative for the lay observer, although the change was probably just a nuisance to railwaymen who knew where Severus was.

It is hard to find any justification for the much more recent change of the name of Poppleton Junction to Skelton for the signal box at the divergence of the Harrogate line unless indeed someone wanted to show that he was years ahead of anyone else in anticipating the closure of that line and that his authority was superior to the physical fact that the junction is further from Skelton than from any of the Poppletons. It is true that there is something slightly comic about the place-name 'Poppleton' and some York residents used to make bucolic jokes about 'Poppleton treacle-mines' many years before there was a sugar-beet factory at Poppleton to provide some faint justification for such imagery.

Beningbrough station was four times as far from Beningbrough village as it was from the much larger village of Shipton but perhaps the latter name was rejected for fear of confusion with the Shipton station on the Great Western in Oxfordshire.

For three furlongs south of Beningbrough station a public road lies alongside the line on the east side and this was convenient for anyone who wanted to be close to a North Eastern train going at top speed. Looking back, one marvels at the success with which the heavy goods traffic of North Eastern times was kept clear of the fast passenger trains on this largely two-track main line. About six miles of four tracks extended from Beningbrough to Alne. From that station to Green Lane just short of Thirsk, train-control was governed by 'Hall' automatic signals worked by compressed carbon dioxide and track circuits. Their arms moved with solemn deliberation, and would sometimes change from 'on' to 'off' for no apparent reason, and immediately go slowly back again.

Railway-lovers when travellers by a road that in general runs parallel to a railway must often have been saddened by the paucity of places from which trains can be conveniently seen from the road. The road from York to Easingwold is mostly within half a mile of the North Eastern main line but from only two points (near Beningbrough and near Tollerton station) are trains visible in any detail. Anyone who wishes to do a bit of close train-watching must take a by-road that intersects the route of the line. Most of the intersections are by overbridge which is not an ideal viewpoint unless indeed one likes a head-on view. Underpasses are few, but there is one beneath the North Eastern main line about a mile north of the site of Sessay Station, which is further from the scattered village of Sessay than it is from Dalton, but this, like Shipton, is a name with other railway applications. A cyclist from Easingwold to Thirsk finds himself, when abreast of Sessay, on sharp undulations on spurs of the Hambleton Hills, in marked contrast to the barely perceptible rise of the railway from Raskelf to Sessay.

Between these stations was a Y-junction with a line leading to Gilling, Pickering and Malton. The north junction box was named Sessay Wood, very confusingly inasmuch as Sessay Station was $2\frac{3}{4}$ miles away, with Pilmoor Station intervening, $\frac{3}{4}$ mile away. 'Pilmoor Grange' would have been a more accurate name.

At Pilmoor was the junction with the line from Knaresborough. Pilmoor station was nearly $\frac{1}{2}$ mile from the nearest public road and $1\frac{1}{2}$ miles from the nearest group of houses (Little Sessay) that might be called a village, but in pre-World War I days, it had quite busy periods with passengers changing trains. There still remain traces of a long-abandoned direct line from the Knaresborough direction across the main line to join the Gilling line over $\frac{1}{2}$ mile away. Adjacent to this track, $\frac{1}{2}$ mile to the west of the main line, were four North Eastern signals each with a slotted post embracing the arm, set close together in a line parallel to the main line. To a traveller on that line, the signals suggested some fairly elaborate track layout on the branch line, but in fact there was none. These signals were used as an object for testing eyesight of engine-drivers in special circumstances. If a driver was found to be barely able to pass the normal tests, he might be accepted if he correctly observed the aspects of these signals from points on the track of the old direct line at distances of 1000, 1100 and 1320 yards. The signals were still available for use in 1969.

From Raskelf northwards are intermittent rises at about 1 in 700 till the 'summit' is reached just short of Eryholme Junction with the Richmond branch. There the line is just over 100 ft higher than the level of the stretch from Poppleton Junction to Alne. A hundred feet at once would be a formidable rise, but spread over 26 miles it averages 1 in 1375 which seems mild enough. Even when one remarks that to overcome gravity against this gradient at a speed of 62 mph each ton of train requires 0.27 horse-power, it still seems mild enough. But when one considers that at this speed the other resistances to motion of a passenger train amount to something less than 2 horse-power per ton it is seen that the difference between running up that gradient and down it is quite considerable. Accepting the 2 horse-power given by the Johansen formula (it would not be far wrong for North Eastern coaching stock) each ton requires 2.27 h.p. going up or 1.73 h.p. coming down, a difference of some 27 per cent. So a 100 ton combination of tender and engine that could average 62 mph from Raskelf to Eryholme with a 300 ton train could make the same speed in the opposite direction with a train of 425 tons. With the 300 ton train it could come down at 70 mph.

Very numerous lineside observations by the writer using timing lengths measured with the aid of Ordnance Survey maps showed that on the Alne-Beningbrough 'level' northbound express passenger trains normally ran at 55 to 62 mph, whilst those in the opposite direction ran at 60 to 68. West winds were common and because they had a strong component across the track were a hindrance to trains in both directions. So the higher speed of the southbound trains on the level was not explained (usually) by wind. The explanation is probably that as the locomotive would come off the train at York and therefore had to pull for only about 10 miles beyond Alne, a driver running slightly late at that point could safely 'open out' the engine without any risk of serious loss of time if she 'ran out of breath'. Many observations from trains show the highest speed between Darlington and York to have been obtained on the final level rather than on the earlier downgrades.

The writer once made a very interesting observation in the course of a journey by bicycle after dark from Easingwold to Boroughbridge. It was ideally windless but unusually dark, dark enough indeed for an oil-lamp to cast a useful light on the road whereas one's normal illumination was starlight or more often cloud reflection of the light from urban areas. But this night was black. As Kipling wrote of entirely different circumstances, 'We moved in the very womb of night', and in due course, having passed Raskelf village, I came to the rise to the bridge over the main line immediately south of Sessay Wood junction. I paused for a moment because here was a railway, although nothing was to be seen. But I did hear the sound of a train running somewhere to the south. In my approach to the bridge. I had seen nothing go south and so the train I could hear was probably coming towards me. It seemed to be a long way off, but I could wait for it. When it got nearer (although still not close) I could hear the front wheels of the engine strike each pair of rail-joints. So why not time the train? While I looked at the seconds hand of my watch by lamp light I counted the rail lengths and before the train reached me I had noted 76 mph which seemed rather fast. The train passed with a white flash from the footplate and a trail of dimmer lights from the coaches. The last wheels hit the rail joints as audibly as the bogie wheels had done. So I took another check on the speed and found only 64 mph. Even though the train had run onto a slight up-grade, its speed would not have dropped by 12 mph in that short time. Why the apparent difference?

Then I thought of the Döppler effect by which the time taken for sound to reach the observer causes an approaching source of periodic sound to seem to be working at a higher frequency than it really is, and of course the opposite effect for a receding source.

A bit of algebra shows that, assuming the train to have run at the same speed during my observations, that speed was twice the product of 76 and 64 divided by their sum. This works out at $69\frac{1}{2}$ mph which is credible.

But the same algebra also shows that the speed of sound on that windless night was twice the product of 76 and 64 divided by their difference and this gives 810 mph which is not a long way from the actual 750 mph. But this is a rather sensitive method of finding the speed of sound; had I noted 77 instead of 76 the answer would have been within one per cent of being correct!

In the ordinary way Class Z 'Atlantics' with fast passenger trains not usually much exceeding 300 tons in weight gave no impression of working hard. When more heavily loaded and running in a strong cross wind they made it clear that they were not liking it very much. Class V 'Atlantics' were noisier. Class R 4-4-0s were confined to the lighter trains and usually ran fast and quietly. All the engines were beautifully clean and made a gleaming head-piece for any train. Their gay colours were in contrast to the blackness of North Western engines on the West Coast main-line, where engines were plainly audible especially when a 4-4-0 was making a running average of over 55 mph with a 450 ton train.

Natural concentration of interest in the locomotive left little time to examine the composition of any fast passenger train. North Eastern coaches were dark red in colour and many had clerestory roofs. 'East Coast Joint Stock' was of Great Northern origin, in varnished teak with bowed ends. These classes of vehicle formed the bulk of the main-line trains but coaches of other companies could also be seen. For example, although not on the main line, a train of North Western coaches, usually Class R hauled, came daily from Harrogate towards Northallerton but kept to the low level line and ran under the main line on its way from Liverpool to Newcastle through Stockton, West Hartlepool and Sunderland.

The numerous goods trains were taken along at about 25 mph by 0-6-0s of the younger varieties and by Class T2 0-8-0s which might take up to seventy loaded wagons. To the youthful eye, goods trains were less interesting than the 'flyers' but now one feels that that ought not to have been so. It is now hard to believe that every goods vehicle carried the initials of its owners in prominent characters. Most of the owners were railway companies, but not all; many collieries had their own wagons appropriately inscribed. So any goods train was worth looking at for one reason or another. Empty vehicles would no doubt depress North Eastern shareholders, but less fortunate spectators could overlook those unavoidable blemishes in a moving picture of commerce.

Yes! The North Eastern main line in the Plain of York was a channel of multi-coloured interest in a pleasant countryside overlooked by beckoning hills. Kilburn White Horse remains serene on its hillside. Away from roads, the hills and the Plain also remain serene. But North Eastern steam is seen no more.

CHAPTER 12

DIMENSIONS

ENTHUSIASTIC students of railway lore sometimes ask what was the use of the published lists of dimensions of locomotives. The answer is that despite their inevitable inaccuracies they do give some idea of the relative sizes of locomotives and from some of them one may make estimates of maximum pull and potential power of different classes.

Looking back, one finds that the diameter of the driving wheels was the figure that first attracted attention. Such a remark as a '7 ft bogie passenger locomotive' was common in early references to locomotives, and that kind of thing was probably the origin of the apparent belief that there could be something quite magical in a particular diameter of driving wheel.

Then came diameter and stroke of the pistons. Everyone could see that these had some influence on the rotation of the driving wheels, but so had steam pressure, and so the working pressure of the boiler came to be mentioned. And so it went on and some enthusiasts began to study the increasing arrays of figures and to use them in calculations purporting to demonstrate this or that. Unfortunately a tendency to hair-splitting arose in examining the results of such calculations and it was a long time before anyone pointed out what a wide range of uncertainty there is in most of the published figures.

In most cases the figures given have an uncertainty of about 5 per cent in each direction. In some instances (eg axle-loading) this may be exceeded in practice. Journey times have a much smaller uncertainty simply because even an ordinary watch has far higher precision than most other methods of obtaining information. It is easy to overlook this and to assume that all published figures are as precise as clockwork. That is not the case. There is a degree of uncertainty about everything and official figures are not exceptions.

Tables 3 to 6 on pages 194–202, extensive though they are, represent a considerable condensation. This has been effected to reduce the risk of obliterating the story by masses of insignificant detail.

Here are given for each class of locomotive the figures for

G   Grate area (sq ft) because that sets a limit to sustained power.

f   Firebox heating surface to suggest whether the firebox is big enough for complete combustion of the fuel at the highest rate at which it can be burned on the grate.

t   Nominal tractive effort (in thousands of pounds). This is the mean pull that the engine could develop during a revolution of its driving wheels at low speed in full gear with full boiler pressure and enough friction between driving wheels and the rails but none anywhere else. It is a factor in estimating the speed-range over which the output of the boiler can be used at the highest possible efficiency in the cylinders.

w   Adhesion weight (tons) because that sets a limit to the starting pull.

D   Diameter (in) of driving wheels (very small ones lead to much wear and tear at high speed)

p   Working pressure (psi) of boiler (there used to be an unjustifiable tendency to believe that the higher it was the better the engine)

d   Diameter of cylinders (in)

s   Stroke of piston (in)

V   Diameter (in) of piston valves

L   Lap (in) of piston valves

The figures for these dimensions are normally obtained from official sources and are as likely to be affected by clerical errors as any others. Published dimensions show discrepancies arising from re-measurement or re-calculation. Actual dimensions suffer variations from wear in service. So no quoted dimension is proved to be incorrect by the mere discovery of a different version elsewhere.

Some official figures are inconsistent with each other and with the relevant drawings. Some of these imperfections have been corrected in preparing Tables 5 and 6 and so some hitherto time-honoured figures have had to be rejected.

The conventional value for 'nominal tractive effort' is

$$t = 0.425 \text{ (Number of cylinders) } p \, d^2 \, s/D$$

Because re-machining after wear increased d and reduced D, the nominal tractive effort rose as the engine got older. So the value quoted in Tables 5 and 6 for t is the next whole number of thousands of pounds *higher* than the nominal amount.

Replacement boilers were often different from the original ones in tubes and superheater. So figures for heating surface of those items were rarely right for the whole life of a locomotive.

Table I

Some performances on the North Eastern main line between Poppleton Junction and Eryholme 37.3 miles with rise (northbound) of 1 in 1920 average.

Run No	1	2	3	4	5	6	7	8	9
Engine No	732	2013	730	784	1244	1908	798	2114	699
Class†	Z_1(H)	R(W)	4CC(W)	V(W)	R_1(W)	Q(W)	S_2(H)	S_1(W)	V_1(H)
Load (ton)	545	375	475	395	365	320	350	385	340
Average speed (mph)	56	57.8	55.8	66.2	67.2	56	63.8	54	66.2
Direction*	N	N	N	S	S	N	S	N	S
DHP per ton	1.83	1.94	1.82	2.1	2.16	1.83	1.94	1.71	2.1
DHP	1000	725	865	830	790	585	680	655	715
DHP/sq ft	37	35	30	30	30	30	29	28	27

† H=Superheated   W=Not superheated

* N=North-bound   S=South-bound

. Chaloner Whin Junction in 1934. Train approaching on East Coast main line from Selby. Gantry carries NE signals and some LNER upper quadrant signals.

50. T. W. Worsdell
51. Wilson Worsdell

Table 2

Class Z No 722
Load 373 tons empty
Load 400 tons loaded

Miles	Timing point	min sec	mph (a)
0	Newcastle (Central)	0 0	
9.9	Cramlington	14 45	40.3
16.6	Morpeth*	21 15	61.8
25.6	Chevington	30 40	57.4
34.8	Alnmouth	38 55	66.9
39.4	Little Mill	43 50	60.0
43.0	Christon Bank	47 30	59.6
46.0	Chathill	50 00	72.0
51.6	Belford	55 30	61.2
58.6	Beal	61 30	70.0
65.7	Tweedmouth	68 40	59.5
66.9	Berwick	70 10	48.0
72.5	Burnmouth	78 35	38.6
74.1	Ayton	80 30	50.3
78.1	Reston	84 30	60.0
83.2	Grantshouse	91 05	55.2
87.9	Cockburnspath	95 30	64.1
90.6	Innerwick	97 50	69.6
95.2	Dunbar	101 55	67.5
106.6	Drem	113 50	57.4
111.2	Longniddry	118 40	57.1
117.9	Inveresk	125 20	60.3
121.4	Portobello	129 00	57.1
124.4	Edinburgh (Waverley)	132 55	46.0

* Speed restriction to 40 mph

(a) Average speed from preceding timing-point

Table 3

Boilers

Grate area sq ft	Firebox length in	Barrel dia. in	Barrel length in	Heating Surfaces (sq ft) Firebox	Tubes	Super- heater	Used in Class
6.3	—*			36	148		K (original)
10.8	46	44	62	45	350		K (no dome)
11.2	52	44	80	57	450		H H1 H2 (no dome)
11.3	48	46	120	75	700		66 (1902)
11.4	50	40	114	85	765		492 (1864)
12.1	52	44	120	82	660		44 (1881) E E1
12.7	54	51	126	84	980		BTP (1874) 124 (1881) 290 (1899)
13.3	57	51	135	93	1150		190 (1894)
13.5	57	51	168	95	1485		1001 (1864)
14.3	60	51	127	90	990		957 (1902)
14.4	60	47	130	120	1100		238 (1871)
15.8	66	51	123	98	994		8 38 901 1440 A G L O P
16.8	70	51	127	98	1090		398 1463
17.3	78	51	127	110	1126		B B1 C C1 I N P1 U
17.3/1	78	51	127	112	1211		D F F1
17.3/2	78	51	127	112	795	263	F F1
19.7	81	52	135	121	1220		M M1 Q
19.7/1	81	52	135	123	790	200	M1 Q
20.5/1	84	51	127	123	1040		J Rebuilt J
20.5/2	84	52	138	127	1099		Q1
20.5/3	84	57	138	144	1380		R
20.5/4	84	57	138	139	1000	227	R
20.5/5	84	66	127	134	1450		P2 P3
22.0	90	57	180	125	1550		T T1
23.7/1	96	54	138	118	1210		3 CC

*Marine-type boiler

Table 3—continued

23.7/2	96	57	132	130	1210		W W1 X
23.7/3	96	57	180	130	1640		S
23.7/4	96	57	190	130	1740		S1
23.7/5	96	66	132	140	1510		Y
23.7/6	96	66	180	144	1226	545	D (1913) S2 T2
27.0	108	66	180	180	2275		V V1
29.0/1	108	60	180	180	1780		4CC
27.0/2	108	66	138	158	1580		R1
27.0/3	108	66	138	158	1160	258	R1
27.0/4	108	66	190	166	1400	530	S3 T3 Z
41.5	96	72	252	200	2170	510	4–6–2

Table 4

Piston valves

Dia. (in) V	Lap (in) L	Lead (in)	Used in Class*
7½	1.375	0.06	Reb.C D (1913) Y Z 4CC
8	1.25	0.13	Rebuilt G I J
8¾	1.125	0.13	R S1 S3 T T3 V W W1 X 4–6–2
10	1.125	0.13	R1 S2 T2 V V1 4CC
13	0.875	?	238

*as first built

A steam-chest designed to take piston valves of any particular diameter could accommodate valves of any smaller diameter or indeed of any slightly larger diameter. So no table such as this can give any more than general guidance based on tradition. There is no guarantee that any locomotive actually complied with the table. There is no possibility of proving that any engine never did so at any time in its life.

Notes on Tables 5 and 6

Letters on particular lines in the table have specific meanings, thus,

Line	Letter	Meaning
2	C	Compound engine
5	BFMT	Indicates the responsible engineer*
3		Number following + refers to engines built after 1922
7		The figure for grate area identifies the boiler in Table 3
16	F	Flat valves
16	P	Piston valves. The preceding figure identifies the valve in Table 4.
17	abc etc.	Letter refers to Fig 6 p. 129
18	J	Joy valve-gear
18	R	With rocking shafts
18	S	Stephenson link-motion
18	Z	With lateral offset

* B **W. Bouch**
 F **E. Fletcher**
 M **A. McDonnell**
 T **H. Tennant**

T. W. Worsdell was responsible for classes first built in 1886–1890
Wilson Worsdell was responsible for classes first built in 1891–1910
Vincent L. Raven was responsible for classes first built after 1910

First building dates of classes with non-standard designations.

6-coupled 6-wheelers (Table 5)		Other Classes (Table 6)	
Class	Date	Class	Date
8	1885	BTP	1874
44	1881	3CC	1898
59	1883	4CC	1906
124	1881	38	1884
290	1899	66	1902
398	1872	190	1894
1001	1864	238	1871
		492	1864
		901	1872
		957	1902
		1440	1875
		1463	1885
		4-6-2	1922

The lists locate the classes (which appear in date order) in Tables 5 and 6

Table 5

Dimensions of Six-coupled Six-wheeled Locomotives

		1001	398	59	C	C1	P	P1	P2	P3
1 NE Class		1001	398	59	C	C1	P	P1	P2	P3
2 Wheel arrangement		060	060	060	Co60	060	060	060	060	060
3 LNE Class		1001	398	J22		J21	J24	J25	J26	J27
4 Number built		56	335	44	171	30	70	120	50	105
5 Date first built		1864B	1872F	1883M	1886	1886	1894	1898	1904	1906
6 Date last built		1875	1883	1885	1892	1895	1898	1902	1905	1923
7 Grate area	G	13.3	16.8	15.8	17.3	17.3	15.6	17.3	20.5/5	20.5/5
8 NTE (1000 lb)	T	13	16	15	18	15	19	22	25	25
9 Adhesion weight (ton)	w	35	38	37	42	42	39	40	48	50
10 Total weight (ton)		35	38	37	42	42	39	40	48	50
11 Tender weight (ton)		18	29	27	37	37	35	36	38	38
12 Boiler pressure (psi)	p	130	160	140	160	140	160	160	180	180
13 Cylinder diameter	d	17	17	17	18/26	18	18	18½	18½	18½
14 Piston stroke	s	24	24	26	24/24	24	24	26	26	26
15 Driving whl. dia.	D	60	60	61	61	61	55	55	55	55
16 Valve type		F	F	F	F	F/7½P	F/7½P	F/7½P	F	F/7½P
17 Cylinder arrgt. p 129		a	a	a	d	b/f	a/f	a/f	a	a/f
18 Valve gear		S	S	S	J	J/S	S/S	S/SZ	S	S/SZ
19 Main description page		41	43	44	45	45	46	46	46	46
20 Illustration facing page		—	—	33	48	—	97	—	97	97

Table 5—continued

		44	124	8	E	H1	L	H2	E1	290
1 NE Class		44	124	8	E	H1	L	H2	E1	290
2 Wheel arrangement		060ST	060T	060T	060T	060CT	060T	060T	060T	060T
3 LNE Class		44	J76	J74	J71	J78	J73	J79	J72	J77
4 Number built		5	10	8	120	2	10	3	75+38	60
5 Date first built		1881	1881	1885	1886	1888	1891	1897	1898	1899
6 Date last built		1883	1882	1885	1895	1888	1892	1897	1921/51	1921
7 Grate area	G	12.1	12.7	15.8	12.1	11.3	15.8	11.3	12.1	12.7
8 NTE (1000 lb)	T	14	15	15	13/17	11	20	11	17	16
9 Adhesion weight (ton)	w	25	41	43	37	27	47	25	39	42
10 Total weight (ton)		25	41	43	37	27	47	25	39	42
11 Tender weight (ton)		—	—	—	—	—	—	—	—	—
12 Boiler pressure (psi)	p	140	140	140	140	140	160	140	140	140
13 Cylinder diameter	d	16	17	17	16/17	14	19	14	17	17
14 Piston stroke	s	24	24	24	22/24	20	24	20	24	22
15 Driving whl.dia.	D	54	54	55	55/49	42	61	41	49	49
16 Valve type		F	F	F	F	F	F	F	F	F
17 Cylinder arrgt. p 129		a	a	a	a	a	b	a	a	a
18 Valve gear		S	S	S	S	S	J	S	S	S
19 Main description page		47	47	47	48	48	48	49	48	48
20 Illustration facing page		—	—	—	49	—	96	—	—	33

Table 6

Dimensions of Locomotives other than Six-coupled Six-wheelers

	492	238	901	BTP	1440	38	1463	A	B	B1	D	F1	F
1 NE Class	492	238	901	BTP	1440	38	1463	A	B	B1	D	F1	F
2 Wheel arrangement	440	2/440	240	044WT	240	440	240	242T	C/062T	062T	C/240	440	C/440
3 LNE Class	—	—	E6	G6	1440	38	E5	F8	—	N8	—	D22	D22
4 Number built	10	10	55	130	15	28	20	60	51	11	2	10	25
5 Date first built	1864F	1871B	1872F	1874F	1875F	1884N	1885T	1886	1886	1886	1886	1886	1887
6 Date last built	1865	1874	1876	1883	1882	1885	1885	1892	1890	1888	1888	1887	1891
7 Grate area (G)	11.4	14.4	15.8	12.7	15.8	15.8	15.8	15.8	17.3	17.3	17.3/1	17.3/1	17.3/1
8 NTE (1000 lb) (T)	11	12	11	11	13	11	11	16	18	20	15	12	15
9 Adhesion weight (ton) (w)													
10 Total weight (ton)	20	28	28	26	27	28	29	28	45	45	31	32	32
11 Tender weight (ton)	29	42	41	46	40	40	42	52	58	58	43	46	47
12 Boiler pressure (psi) (P)	130	140	140	140	160	140	140	160	160	160	175	140	175
13 Cylinder dia. (d)	16	17	17½	16	17	17	18	18	18/26	19	18/26	18	18/26
14 Piston stroke (s)	22	30	24	22	24	24	24	24	24/24	24	24/24	24	24/24
15 Driving whl. dia. (D)	60	85	85	60	73	80	84	67	61	61	80	80	80
16 Valve type	F	13P	F	F	F	F	F	F	F	F	F	F	F
17 Cylinder arrgt. p. 129	a	i	a	a	a	a	a	b	d	b	d	b	d
18 Valve gear	S	S	S	S	S	S	S	J	J	J	J	J	J
19 Main description p.	21	18	50	52	—	25	29	53	53	53	54	55	55
20 Illsuration facing p.	32	32	32	32	—	—	33	48	48	—	48	—	49

Table 6—continued

	G	H	I	J	K	M1	M	N	N	O	Reb.J	Q	Q1
1 NE Class	G	H	I	J	K	M1	M	N	190	O	Reb.J	Q	Q1
2 Wheel arrangement	240	040T	C/422	C/422	040T	440	C/440	062T	224T	044T	422	440	440
3 LNE Class	—	Y7	—	—	Y8	D17/1	—	N9	X3	G5	—	D17/2	D18
4 Number built	20	17+5	10	20	5	20	1	20	2	110	20	30	2
5 Date first built	1887	1888	1888	1889	1890	1892	1893	1893	1894	1894	1894	1896	1896
6 Date last built	1888	1897	1890	1890	1890	1894	1893	1894	1894	1901	1895	1897	1896
7 Grate area G	15.8	11.2	17.3	20.5/1	10.8	19.7	19.7	17.3	13.3	15.8	20.5/1	19.7	20.5/2
8 NTE (1000 lb) T	13	11	15	16	6	17	21	21	10	18	14	17	17
9 Adhesion weight (ton) w	29	25	18	19	16	34	34	45	18	30	19	33	34
10 Total weight (ton)	40	25	44	47	16	51	52	56	49	52	47	50	51
11 Tender weight (ton)	32	—	35	41	—	41	41	—	—	—	41	38	41
12 Boiler pressure (psi) P	160	140	175	175	140	180	200	160	160	160	175	175	175
13 Cylinder dia. d	17	14	18/26	20/28	11	19	19/28	19	16	18	19	19½	20
14 Piston stroke s	24	20	24/24	24/24	15	26	26/26	26	22	24	24	26	26
15 Driving whl dia. D	73	42	85	91	36	85	85	61	78	61	91	85	91
16 Valve type	F	F	F	F	F	F	F	F	F	F	8P	F	F
17 Cylinder arrgt. p 129	b	a	d	e	a	c	e	b	a	a	g	b	b
18 Valve gear	J	S	J	JR	S	JR	JR	SR	S	S	SZ	SR	SR
19 Main description p.	56	58	59	59	62	63	66	54	69	71	62	73	73
20 Illustration facing p	49	—	96	96	—	96	—	—	—	97	—	112	112

Table 6—continued

#	Dimension	3CC	R	S	Reb.I	S1	T/T1	Reb.G	U	66	957	V	4CC	W
1	NE Class	3CC	R	S	Reb.I	S1	T/T1	Reb.G	U	66	957	V	4CC	W
2	Wheel arrangement	3C/440	440	2/460	422	2/460	2/080	440	062T	C224T	224T	2/442	4C/442	460T
3	LNE Class	D19	D20	B13	—	B14	Q5	D23	N10	X1	X2	C6	C8	—
4	Number built	1	60	40	10	5	40/50	20	20	1	1	10	2	10
5	Date first built	1898	1899	1899	1900	1901	1901/2	1901	1902	1902	1902	1903	1906	1907
6	Date last built	1898	1907	1909	1902	1901	1911	1909	1903	1902	1902	1904	1906	1908
7	Grate area G	23·7/1	20·5/3	23·7/3	17·3	23·7/4	22·0	15·8	17·3	11·3	14·3	27·0	29·0/1	23·7/2
8	NTE (1000 lb) T	20	20	24	14	18	28	15	24	8	12	23	29	23
9	Adhesion weight w (ton)	37	36	47	18	52	62	31	44	20	19	39	39	52
10	Total weight (ton)	54	55	63	44	67	62	45	57	45	51	73	74	69
11	Tender weight (ton)	39	39	39	35	40	39	32	—	—	—	44	43	—
12	Boiler pressure (psi)	200	200	200	175	160	175	160	175	175	160	200	225	170
13	Cylinder dia. p	19/20	19	20	18	20	20	18	18½	13/18½	17	20	14½/22	19
14	Piston stroke d	26/24	26	26	24	26	26	24	26	20/20	22	28	26/26	26
15	Driving whl. dia. D s	85	82	73	84	80	55	73	55	68	73	82	85	61
16	Valve type	F/8¾P	8¾P	F	8P	8¾P	8¾P/F	8P	8P	F	F	10P	7½P/10P	8¾P
17	Cylinder arrgt.	j	f	h	g	i	i/h	g	f	a	a	i	k	f
18	Valve gear	S/SZ	SZ	S	SZ	S	S	SZ	SZ	S	S	S	SR/SR	SZ
19	Main description p.	66	74	84	62	88	92	56	54	69	69	96	81	100
20	Illustration facing p.	161	112	113	—	113	144	—	145	33	—	145	161	160

p 129

Table 6—continued

	R1	X	V1	Y	S2	Z	D(1913)	T2	W1	S3	T3	4-6-2
1 NE Class	R1	X	V1	Y	S2	Z	D(1913)	T2	W1	S3	T3	4-6-2
2 Wheel arrangement	440	3/480T	2/442	3/462T	2/460	3/442	3/444T	2/080	462T	3/460	3/080	3/462
3 LNE Class	D21	T1	C6	A7	B15	C7	H1	Q6	A6	B16	Q7	A2
4 Number built	10	10+5	10	20	20	50	45	120	10	38+32	5+10	2+3
5 Date first built	1908	1909	1910	1910	1911	1911	1913	1913	1914	1919	1919	1922
6 Date last built	1909	1909/25	1910	1911	1913	1918	1921	1921	1917	1922/24	1919/24	1922/24
7 Grate area G	27.0/2	23.7/2	27.0	23.7/5	23.7/6	27.0/4	23.7/2	23.7/6	23.7/2	27.0/4	27.0/4	41.5
8 NTE (1000 lb) T	22	34	20	30	22	18	21	26	23	30	38	30
9 Adhesion weight (ton) W	42	67	40	56	53	40	40	66	48	59	73	60
10 Total weight (ton)	60	85	76	87	71	77	85	66	78	78	73	97
11 Tender weight (ton)	41	—	41	—	39	45	—	39	—	46	44	46
12 Boiler pressure (psi)	225	175	180	180	180	160	160	160	170	180	180	200
13 Cylinder dia. p/d	19	18	19½	16½	20	16½	16½	20	19	18½	18½	19
14 Piston stroke s	26	26	26	26	26	26	26	26	26	26	26	26
15 Driving whl.dia. D	82	55	82	55	73	82	69	55	61	68	55	80
16 Valve type	10P	8¾P	10P	7½P	10P	7½P	7½P	10P	8¾P	8¾P	8¾P	8¾P
17 Cylinder arrgt.			i	m	i	m	m	i	f	m	m	m
18 Valve gear p 129	g / SZ	m / S/SR	S	S/SR	S	S/SZ	S/SZ	S	SZ	S/SZ	S/SZ	S/SZ
19 Main description p.	78	105	96	107	90	108	112	93	103	90	95	114
20 Illustration facing p	112	160	145	160	113	160	49	144	103	144	145	161

CHAPTER 13

CAREERS

The following notes summarize published information about the careers of the men who were successively in charge of the locomotives of the North Eastern Railway from its formation in 1854 till its absorption in the LNER in 1923.

Edward Fletcher

1809 born

1829 Assisted in trials of Stephenson's *Rocket* at Killingworth

1830 Canterbury & Whitstable Railway

1832 York & North Midland Railway

1845 Locomotive Superintendent, Newcastle & Darlington Railway

1854 Locomotive Superintendent, North Eastern Railway

1882 Retired

1889 died

Alexander McDonnell

1830 born

1852 Graduated with honours at the University of Dublin

1865 Locomotive & Wagon Superintendent, Great Southern & Western Railway (Ireland)

1883 Locomotive Superintendent, North Eastern Railway

1884 Resigned

T. W. Worsdell

1837 born, Son of N. Worsdell, Carriage Superintendent of Grand Junction Railway
Many jobs in his early working years

1865 Altoona works of Pennsylvania Rail Road

1868 Master Mechanic at Altoona

1871 Works Manager, Crewe (LNWR)

1881 Locomotive Superintendent, Great Eastern Railway

1885 Locomotive Superintendent, North Eastern Railway

1890 Retired (ill health)

1916 died (at Arnside, Westmorland)

Wilson Worsdell

1850 born at Church Coppenhall (near Crewe), brother of T. W. Worsdell
Educated at Society of Friends School at Ackworth, Yorks.

1866 Six months in Drawing Office at Crewe Works (LNWR)

1867 Pupil of Superintendent of Motive Power & Machinery at Altoona Works of Pennsylvania Rail Road

1871 Erecting shop at Crewe

1872 Drawing office at Crewe

1874 Stafford Shed, LNWR

1876 Bushbury Shed, LNWR

1877 In charge of Chester Shed, LNWR

1883 Assistant Locomotive Superintendent, North Eastern Railway

1890 Locomotive Superintendent, North Eastern Railway

1902 Title changed to Chief Mechanical Engineer

1910 Retired

1920 died

Vincent Litchfield Raven

1859 born at Great Fransham, Norfolk, son of Rector
      Educated at Aldenham School, Herts.

1877 Pupil of Edward Fletcher, North Eastern Railway

1893 Assistant Mechanical Engineer, North Eastern Railway

1910 Chief Mechanical Engineer, North Eastern Railway

1915 Superintendent, Royal Arsenal, Woolwich.

1917 Awarded KBE

1923 Technical Adviser, LNER

1924 Resigned

1934 died

INDEX

Bridge of Earn, 96
Brougham class, 17, 20
Brunel, I. K., 29
Buffered-up vehicles, 172
Bulleid, O. V. S., 19
Burton Salmon, 15, 171

Cabs
  bad, 84
  clerestory roof, 73, 180
  commodious, 17
  elemental, 17
  hot, 32, 73
  living conditions, 31, 32
  low roof, 98
  rabbit-hutch, 31
  side-window, 30, 31
  ventilation, 73, 176
Cab fittings (Class M1), 137
Cab signalling, 145
Carbonisation of oil, 144
Carbutt, Sir E. H., 123
Carlisle, 15
Cataract cylinder, 142
'Cauliflower', 44
Centenary, Stephenson, 22
Chaloner Whin Junction, 180
  facing 192
Changing enginemen, 27
Char-ejector, 110
Cheating, 112
Chester-le-Street, 64
Chimney, 29
  brass-rimmed, 16, 73, 93, 111
  cast iron, 111
  stove-pipe, 20
  facing 32
Church Fenton, 62, 172, 175, 176, 177
Churchward, G. J., 37, 79, 102
Classes of locomotives—*See* pp 197–202
  and
'Claughton' (LNW), 111
Clearance volume, 135

Coal-consumption, 45, 53, 64, 66, 75, 93, 96, 101, 121, 123, 134, 151
Coal depots, 178
Coal dust nuisance, 105
Cockburnspath, 87, 193
Coke, 20
Colton Bridge, 179
Compounding, 33, 124
  economy, 45, 125, 128
Compound engines,
  2-cyl., 126
  3-cyl., 67
  4-cyl., 38, 81
  starting, 125, 130
Condenser, 125
Connecting rods, 91, 107, 111
Copmanthorpe, 180
Cost, running, 151, 152
Counter-pressure locomotive, 88
Crank-axle, 92
Crewe Works, 30, 36, 204
Crosshead, 106
Cross water-tubes, 67
Croxdale, 106
Crudity, 22, 29, 97
Curves
  negotiation of, 65
Cylinder block, 34, 107
  cocks, 144
  covers, burst, 19
  outside, 92
Classes of locomotives
  A, 30, 52
  B, 31, 33, 53
  B1, 31, 53, 101
  BTP, 52
  C, 45
  C1, 45, 177
  D (1886), 54
  D (1913), 39, 112
    performance (No. 2145), 114
  E, 48

roundabout, 61
Stévart, 130
Walschaerts, 82, 91, 130, 133
Vibration, 100, 117

Wagons, 178, 187
Waste, 25
Water, 153
-crane, 159
-tube, cross, 67
-wall, 19
'Waterburys' (Class G), 56
extraordinary effort, 57
Waterworks Signal Box, 158
Wath, 39, 105
-tanks, 39, 105, 107
Watson, H. A., 64
Watson, T. C., 96
Wear, 20
Weatherboard, 21
Webb, F. W., 26
Weight-transfer, 105
Well-tank engines, 9, 52
Westinghouse pump, 36, 71, 169
coal-activated, 36
Wetherby, 102
Whale, G., 36
Wharfe, River, 177

Wheel-base, symmetrical, 113
'Whitby bogies' (Class 492), 21
Willy (Class W), 102
Wind, 148, 154, 159, 185
Woolly Willy (Class W1), 103
Worsdell Gobblers, 53
Worsdell, T. W., 30, 45, 53–62, 124
facing 193, 204
Worsdell Wilson, 34, 46, 62–108
facing 193, 204
Works, locomotive
Darlington, 25, 32, 69
Doncaster, 69, 181
Gateshead, 24
Horwich, 179, 181
Inchicore, 25
Leeds, 24
Swindon, 79
York, 24

York, 15, 147, 170
Museum, 22, 71, 139
railway archives, 8
re-manning at, 27
starting from, 181
station pilots, 182
York-Darlington, 82, 147, 160
York Yard North, 182